MODERN
DANCE

About the author

A native of Chicago, Esther E. Pease completed most of her formal education in California, taking both bachelor's and master's degrees at the University of California at Los Angeles. In California she taught at Whittier College and the University of California at San Diego. Later she completed a Ph.D. at the University of Michigan.

As one of the first women to enter military service during World War II, she graduated from Officers Training School at Ft. Des Moines and later from Command and General Staff School at Leavenworth. After four years service as WAC Staff Director for the Air Force Weather Service, she returned to civilian life to resume study and teaching, first at Purdue University and then at the University of Michigan, where she was chairman of the dance program and introduced the first four-year dance major in the state of Michigan, as well as a graduate dance program.

She studied dance with Mary Wigman in Dresden and Berlin in Germany; with Kurt Jooss in England; and with Martha Graham, Doris Humphrey, Hanya Holm, Charles Weidman, Louis Horst, and others in the United States.

She has held numerous offices including state dance chairman for California, Indiana, and Michigan; national research chairman and national dance chairman for the AAHPER; consultant and field reader for the Department of Health, Education, and Welfare; member of the dance committee of the Michigan Council for the Arts; co-chairman for the Bi-National Dance Conference between the United States and Canada. She has contributed to numerous publications on dance as well as being coauthor of *Modern Dance: Building and Teaching Lessons*.

She retired early from the University of Michigan to free-lance as choreographer, teacher, and lecturer on dance, to pursue the study of watercolor and duplicate bridge, and to travel. Recently she was choreographer for the University of Michigan production of *Pericles*, starring Nicholas Pennel of the Stratford Shakespeare Festival Players.

MODERN DANCE

Dance Series

Esther E. Pease

Illustrations by the author

Second Edition

Wm C Brown Company Publishers
Dubuque, Iowa

Photographs courtesy of the Department
of Dance, The University of Michigan

Consulting Editor

Aileene Lockhart
Texas Woman's University

Evaluation Materials Editor

Jane A. Mott
Smith College

Copyright © 1966, 1976 by Wm. C. Brown Company Publishers

Library of Congress Catalog Card Number: 75-23607

ISBN 0—697—07068—9

Printed in the United States of America

Contents

· Preface vii

1. Why dance? 1

2. The emergence of modern dance 4

3. A view of you 11

4. For men only 17

5. The studio experience 21

6. Working with basic principles 25

7. Techniques 32

8. Stretch your imagination 39

9. On being creative 43

10. Movement by design 50

11. Notes on performing 61

12. Looking at dance 65

13. Two on the aisle 70

14. Pilgrim's progress 75

   A basic vocabulary 77

   A suggested reading list 79

   What do you think? 82

   Appendix: Questions and answers 84

   Index 87

Preface

Why dance? What will it do for me? How does it relate to my life-style and my chosen field of study? Will it be a good investment of the time and effort it requires? Am I likely to be successful? Probably you have been asking yourself these or similar questions if you are considering enrolling in a modern dance class. Most beginners do.

This book about modern dance is designed to provide you with some of the answers, to better prepare you for the challenge of a new experience, and to accompany your dance study. It will not take the place of a good instructor, but it should help you get more from your study.

You might not take more than one beginning dance class, but through it you will acquire basic knowledge and skills in the effective use of your body that will remain with you for the rest of your life. In addition, you will become a better audience for dance following your experience. You will have a better understanding of the way a professional dancer prepares himself, and you will also know more about the creative process that leads to a choreographed dance work. And who knows? This experience might cause you to chart a new life for yourself as a dancer! There is an ancient Chinese proverb that states: A journey of a thousand miles is begun when you take the first step.

May your first step bring you joy!

Esther E. Pease

Why dance?

1

loos'd of limits
and imaginary lines
I am larger, better than I thought.
"Song of the Open Road"
by Walt Whitman

Being gregarious by nature, men and women have sought the companionship of others since the beginning of time. Even before there were permanent towns and villages, they established stable relationships with other human beings by living together in small family units. Eventually, several families joined together to form a tribe, united by a common ancestry and customs.

As their societal structure became more complex, people had an increased need to communicate with other members of their family and tribe. Grunts began to evolve into word symbols, and random movements grew into meaningful gestures. Gradually, primitive people acquired the ability to express themselves by using a basic language of sounds and motions.

In addition to the need to communicate, some individual members of the tribe began to seek ways to express the intensity of their experiences. They began to organize sounds into melodies and words into chants. They carved ornaments to decorate their bodies and they recorded their deeds, painting them upon the walls of caves. They gave expression to their feelings by dancing. This marked the beginning of art.

As our early ancestors moved forward in time, they began to preserve certain aspects of their culture. Movement patterns began to be repeated upon certain occasions until they became rituals that were handed down from father to son and mother to daughter. These rituals were based upon meaningful rhythmic movements of the body through which people believed they could communicate with their gods or celebrate the memorable events of their lives. There were specific rituals requesting assistance from the gods to assure the success of the hunt, to give them the strength to ward off their enemies, to cure their ailments, and subdue the wrath of nature when there were floods, storms, and earthquakes. These we have classified as rites of intensification or rituals, wherein people sought the assistance of their gods.

Rites of passage were also performed to commemorate the important phases of life such as birth, the onset of puberty, the union of a marriage, or the passage from life to the mystery of death. The patterns became fixed and preserved from generation to generation.

During each successive stage of cultural development, man has danced. Even when prohibited by law and edict, denounced by emperors and popes, banned from village greens and marketplaces, or banished from courts and cathedrals (there were danced Masses), dance, inherent in the nature of man, could not be destroyed. Because of the need to communicate through movement, to give expression to thoughts and feelings, dance has been in existence throughout the ages. "Dancing is body talk"[1] and fulfills a basic need to express the self.

Children contain the seeds of dance. Observe how spontaneously they move and how they delight in giving vent to their moods through the unrestricted use of their bodies. Through their uninhibited rhythmic responses they often give outward expression to inner feelings. They delight in the discovery of new ways of moving; they improvise, imitate, repeat, change patterns, and invent with obvious rapture. Unless restricted by an adult hand, they do not maintain a sedate walk for long; they caper, jump, hop, skip, and scamper. They seldom follow the most direct route. Instead, they zig and zag, stop, twist and turn, and go in reverse in an ever-changing filigree of arcs and angles. Their patterns and their forms of locomotion are as changeable as the wind. Their responses are visible evidence of what they see, feel, and hear in their world.

One autumn day I watched from my living room window as a small child played among the leaves that had fallen upon the lawn. Using her feet, she drew them into swirling patterns; she kicked them into the air; she scooped up handfuls of the brilliant colors and scattered them in all directions; she tried to catch them as they fell. Gathering a leafy bouquet in each hand, she started to turn, spinning slowly at first and then with increasing speed.

---

1. Sylvia Ashton-Warner, *Teacher* (New York: Simon and Schuster, 1963), p. 55.

As she whirled faster and faster, I began counting the revolutions—twenty ... thirty ... forty—as she spun on and on. Suddenly she stopped still for a brief moment, her body poised on tiptoe and stretching skyward. Then intoxication took command, and staggering and lurching across the lawn while she laughed at the deliciously dizzying experience, she tumbled down into a bed of leaves and rested momentarily. She had participated in that autumn day; she had been attuned to it and had given expression in her own way, freely and delightfully.

Through dance you arrive at the core of your own individuality. As you gain the control and mastery of the movements your physical body is capable of making, your body becomes the vehicle for the expression of your true self. Dance is affirmative, the positive and dynamic statement of who and what you really are. As soon as you have attained the discipline of even a small part of it, when you are able to perform a series of turns or leaps or a spiral fall and recovery—yes, even a good *grand plié*—you will sense this affirmation, this feeling of inner harmony. This is a taste of the personal ecstacy that all dancers experience when they perform well. Work toward the moments when, as James Angell has written "life is celebrated, tasted, lived, spent, painted, danced, shared, and set to music—all under the banner of some innate, imperishable yes. . . ."[2]

The urge to dance lies locked within all of us. It can be released through participation and developed through good instruction. In its maturity it becomes art, but only after it has been shaped and molded into what Suzanne Langer refers to as significant form.[3] It perpetuates a long tradition, bringing a further enrichment to our own culture. It is your heritage and your birthright.

2. James W. Angell, *Yes Is a World* (Waco, Texas: Word Book, 1974).
3. Suzanne K. Langer, *Feeling and Form* (New York: Charles Scribner's Sons, 1953), p. 24.

The emergence of modern dance

2

Modern or contemporary dance is a part of the cultural explosion that changed the shape of all the arts during the twentieth century. Its creation was inevitable, not accidental, for, as Clive Bell pointed out, "art is a reflection of its time."[1] It mirrors the present, not in a literal sense but as a commentary about our relationship to the present. We all are products of our particular time; we can dwell neither in the past nor in the future. What has passed often has given roots to tradition or provided a storehouse into which we can dip when we want to look backward. We also are incapable of predicting the future, unless we believe in horoscopes or crystal-ball gazing. There is an immediacy to art that is in keeping with the here and now. Note the difference between a portrait by Picasso and one by Rembrandt, or contrast a musical composition by Stravinsky to the music of Mozart. Each was appropriate for the time in which it was composed, but the times were not the same. When the materials, tools, and subject matter no longer are suitable for the reflection of the immediate present, the artist finds new avenues to explore.

At the start of the twentieth century, the acceptable art form of dance

1. Clive Bell, *Art* (London: Chatto and Windus, 1914).

was classical ballet, a style of dancing that had changed very little from the time of its origins during the seventeenth and eighteenth centuries. Its movements were aristocratic and noble, as befitted the manners and actions of those born to dwell in royal palaces. Its codified gestures, attitudes, and steps were suited to the actions of dancers cast in the roles of lords and ladies, nymphs and satyrs, gods and goddesses. The dances were performed against backgrounds representing woodland glades, pastoral meadows, castle ballrooms, or imaginary Mount Olympuses. As an art, dance had been standing still for three hundred years, so enslaved by tradition that it had not kept pace with the other arts. Painting, music, and poetry were in the process of discovering new frontiers even before the turn of the century, but dance had lagged behind.

The first dance rebel to break away from the traditions of the classical ballet was Isadora Duncan (1878-1927) whose childhood years were spent in San Francisco but whose talents later were recognized and acclaimed by European audiences. As a child she was taken to study with a famous ballet teacher since she evidenced a talent for dancing at an early age. After a few lessons, however, Isadora refused to return to the class. In her autobiography, *My Life*, she described her reactions:

When the teacher told me to stand on my toes I asked him why, and when he replied "Because it is beautiful" I said that it was ugly and against nature and after the third lesson I left his class, never to return. The stiff and commonplace gymnastics which he called dancing only disturbed my dreams. I dreamed of a different dance.[2]

Isadora explored many new ideas and places in her search for this "different dance." She discovered the poetry of Walt Whitman, particularly the collection *Leaves of Grass*. Later, during a journey to Greece, she became enamored of its ancient classical beauty and sought to express this beauty through dance. She designed dances of her own and presented them to audiences throughout the entire European continent. Finally, after establishing a dancing school for children in Berlin, six of her "Isadorables" toured with her, and after her tragic death in an automobile accident, they attempted to carry on her tradition by opening a school for Duncan Dancers in New York.

There is little similarity between the form and style of Isadora Duncan's dancing and the modern dance we know today. Her movements were too unstructured and too natural by today's standards, and her choreography was too romantically sentimental or too obviously political for present-day tastes. Barefooted, her body draped in diaphanous materials or the French flag, she ran, skipped, knelt, and twirled in front of the ever-present

---

2. Isadora Duncan, *My Life* (New York: Boni and Liveright, 1927), p. 22.

blue curtains that became her symbol to the music of Gluck, Chopin, Liszt, Tchaikovsky, and the *Marseillaise*. For several years her influence could be observed. A host of barefooted "interpretative dancers" wearing Greek tunics ran, leaped, and skipped, attempting to follow in her path. The modern dancer, however, moves in a disciplined way to contemporary sounds. Our inheritance from Isadora Duncan is limited to her spirit of dynamic action.

Modern dance is directly descended from the innovations of two of the greatest and most influential creative artists of our time—Mary Wigman (1886-1973) and Martha Graham (1894-   ). Mary Wigman, the first modern dancer, began shaping the new dance form in her native country, Germany, at the time of World War I. She began dancing when she was twenty-nine years old, following a brief career as a pianist and an actress. She believed that movement would become the most direct of the arts if it could communicate symbolic expressions of experience, but that its old forms had to be relinquished. Wigman's search for a new dance led her first to Hellerau to the Dalcroze Institute, where a movement system known as Eurhythmy was being taught. Designed specifically to sensitize musicians in order to heighten their responses to rhythm, this system did not entirely meet her needs. Having heard rumors about Rudolph von Laban's experiments with the laws of human motion and his innovation of scales for three-dimensional designs, she went to Anscona, Switzerland to seek his guidance. For several years, first as an apprentice and then as Laban's assistant, Mary Wigman began evolving a method of dance that became known ultimately as the "new German dance" which applied theories of time and motion to the dance art. Laban's later investigations of the subject contributed significantly to the improvement of industrial methods in England during World War II and also to the establishment of a widely used method for recording movement, *Labanotation*. Wigman, however, left Zurich in 1916 to establish her independence as a dance artist and to organize dance centers in Berlin and Dresden where young students could be taught the new modern dance. She toured Frankfurt, Hannover, Munich, and eventually all the important cities of Europe as a soloist and then with her company of dancers, sharing her discoveries with enthusiastic audiences everywhere. Reports of her activities were read in the United States, and they indirectly influenced the development of the American modern dance. (Wigman's first tour of this country was several years after Martha Graham's initial concert.) Her legacy has been summarized by the perceptive dance critic Margaret Lloyd:

With her [Wigman] came new ideas of the dancer's relation to space and the dance's relation to music, of movement evolved out of its own meaning, of dance self-governing and self-contained . . . new music to be written . . . or dispensing with music altogether.[3]

Martha Graham, once described by *Time* magazine as the "high priestess of American dance," was born in a suburb of Philadelphia and began her dancing career only after her family moved to California, where she was permitted to enroll as a student at the Denishawn School in Los Angeles. Named for its cofounders Ruth St. Denis and Ted Shawn, this institution became known as the cradle of American modern dance, for Charles Weidman began his dancing career at Denishawn and Doris Humphrey and Louis Horst were members of its faculty. Each became a pioneer in the development and establishment of modern dance as an independent art. Martha Graham entered Denishawn in 1916 (at that time, Mary Wigman already was composing works for her company) and left in 1923 to appear for two seasons in the Greenwich Village Follies. She did so, at least in part, because she had become dissatisfied with the Oriental mysticism and the overtones of American Indian and Spanish dance that colored the Denishawn expression. In 1925, Graham accepted an invitation to teach dance at the Eastman School of Music in Rochester, and a year later (April 18, 1926, at the Forty-Eighth Street Theater in New York City), she gave her first independent concert. Hailed by one bewildered critic as "The Blessed Damozel," she began the American dance revolution with this public appearance. Other dancers such as Doris Humphrey, Charles Weidman, Helen Tamiris, and Agnes De Mille, spurred on to some extent by the provocative suggestions of Louis Horst (who by this time had become Graham's accompanist, musical director, and catalytic agent), began exploring with movement in new ways and presented concerts whenever they could scrape together enough money to rent a small theater in New York. Hanya Holm, who came to New York shortly after these first revolutionary outbursts, established a branch of the Mary Wigman school but soon felt the urge to relate her style of dance to the American scene. During the 1930s, the "Big Four" studios for dance instruction were established, and companies were formed for concert appearances that crisscrossed the American continent many times (the Graham, Humphrey-Weidman, and Holm organizations).

Modern dance, allying itself with the contemporary movement that had infiltrated poetry, music, painting, sculpture, and architecture, had discovered an idiomatic dance that could reflect the spirit of its time.

Martha Graham's contributions to modern dance probably never can be fully assessed. She has never stood still; with each concert she has re-

3. Margaret Lloyd, *The Borzoi Book of Modern Dance* (New York: Alfred A. Knopf, 1949), p. 16.

vealed new concepts born from her own creativity. She has directed attention to the importance of form, to the necessity of looking within one's self to discover the spiritual source of dance, and to the fact that new techniques arise from the demands of a composition. She has emphasized the contraction-release principle of all body movement and has led us to explore the floor as well as the space above it; she has found ways of propelling the body other than with the feet, using the knees, stomach, and spine. She is insistent, as any good teacher is, that her dancers discipline their bodies and have them under control at all times. Two generations of brilliant dance artists have felt her influence as well as hundreds of dance teachers—Paul Taylor, Pearl Lang, Yuriko, Merce Cunningham, John Butler, Erick Hawkins, Sophie Maslow, and Anna Sokolow are only a few of those who have benefited from their association and study with Martha Graham. John Martin, dean emeritus of American dance criticism, compares Graham's genius and influence to Picasso's painting and Stravinsky's music.

The twentieth century not only gave rise to modern dance, a new art form of dance, but it also altered the design of the ballet, ridding it of its preoccupation with the past. Although the time-honored classical ballets such as *Giselle, Swan Lake, Coppelia,* and *The Nutcracker Suite* were not entirely abandoned, new works based upon contemporary themes updated the performances of ballet companies, particularly in the United States. American ballet choreographers began exploring the facets of our own culture, looking at the contemporary scene and at the legends of our own heritage instead of at the myths and fairy tales of European origin. Agnes de Mille's *Rodeo,* first performed by the Ballet Russe de Monte Carlo in 1933, Catherine Littlefield's *Barn Dance,* choreographed for the Philadelphia Ballet, Ruth Page's *Billy Sunday,* Lew Christensen's *Filling Station,* and Eugene Loring's *Billy the Kid* and *Yankee Clipper* were among the early successful ballets in the new idiom.

With the new themes came changes in conventional ballet techniques. In de Mille's *Fall River Legend,* Lizzie Borden had to come off *pointe* to portray the character of the daughter who wielded the axe so many times. Because of the demands of the new choreographies, ballet had to relinquish its insistence upon perfection of classical techniques and extend its range of movement to include movements similar to those used in modern dance. It has become increasingly difficult today to classify a piece as either ballet or modern. Where, for instance, do we place Jerome Robbins's dances for *West Side Story* or the dances of the sailors on shore leave in *Fancy Free?* Unless one is familiar with the artists' previous backgrounds and training, some of the works by George Ballanchine (ballet) and Merce Cunningham (modern) are difficult to categorize. The gaps between the two art forms of dance no longer are wide, and today it is evident that many techniques have been used by both, although modern dance has yet to adopt the toe shoes of the ballerina, and ballet still emphasizes the rigidity of the spine.

Another development in dance in the present century accompanied the emergence of a purely American form of music, jazz. Jazz dance, with its emphasis upon rhythmic syncopation and open gestures and its carefree quality, has a strong appeal to audiences and has become an important adjunct to theatrical performances particularly in the field of musical comedy. It possesses a style all its own that is exuberant and extroverted most of the time, and it is preoccupied with movement *per se* as opposed to content.

Closely related to jazz dance but more firmly rooted in the soil of Africa are the ethnic dances of the black people. African dance has become increasingly popular with American audiences due to the efforts of individuals such as Pearl Primus, whose original training was in modern dance. Her interest in anthropology sent her back to the land of her ancestors to seek out the dances of some of the tribes in western and central Africa and to adapt them for the American stage. Ethnic dance, which had concentrated for many years upon the folk dances of the countries in western Europe, has begun to focus upon the black heritage in existence in the islands of the Caribbean and our southern states as well as in Africa. Superb dance artists such as Katherine Dunham, Jean Léon Destiné, Talley Beatty, and Geoffrey Holder have enriched the American theater by re-creating and transforming the dances of Haiti, Trinidad, and other places in the West Indies. Alvin Ailey has created superbly moving works such as *Revelations* for his modern dance company which are based upon the spiritual heritage of the southern black people in our nation.

What happened during these developmental years in the schools and colleges of our nation? Until the midthirties, modern dance in education was practically unknown. Those of us in the schools were dancing, however, and not ballet, but what was known as *natural dance*. We wore Greek tunics over tank suits, waved china-silk scarves in the air, and hopped, skipped, ran, and waltzed to the music of Chopin and Grieg. Dance was taught by female physical educators, many of whom were trained by Gertrude Colby at Columbia University.

A few perceptive, intelligent, and persuasive educators began to initiate changes, however, including Margaret H'Doubler at the University of Wisconsin, Ruth L. Murray at Wayne State University, Martha B. Deane at the University of California at Los Angeles, and Martha Hill at New York University. They began to look at dance scientifically and psychologically, to analyze its movements kinesiologically, to use contemporary music instead of the classics, and to encourage their students to be inventive in the design of movement patterns instead of limiting them to learning step patterns. They conducted workshops, organized a national dance section within the National Physical Education Association in 1932, and presented concerts and lecture demonstrations within their communities. Interested students were encouraged to attend concerts given by professional dance artists and to study with the professionals in New York, California, and Germany (Mary Wigman).

The professional dance artists and the educators were brought together through the efforts of Martha Hill and Mary Jo Shelley in 1934 when they organized a summer session to teach modern dance at Bennington College, a liberal arts school in Vermont. Among the faculty were Martha Graham, Doris Humphrey, Charles Weidman, and Louis Horst who, along with members of the professional companies, worked with the dance educators and students in the new concepts and materials of modern dance. Other centers for summer dance study began opening up—Jacob's Pillow in Massachusetts, Perry-Mansfield in Colorado, and Connecticut College for Women (a continuation of the Bennington plan). By the 1940s, modern dance had become established in the curricula of most colleges and universities and in a number of high schools throughout the country.

Soon it became apparent that it was necessary to offer specialized training to provide the schools and colleges with qualified dance teachers. This led to the development of the dance major separate from physical education, and the dance concentrate program within physical education. The Juilliard School in New York City expanded its program to include the study of dance as well as of music, and many of its graduates have been added to the dance faculties of our colleges and universities.

In recent years there has been a noticeable trend toward relocating the administration of dance on the college campus to ally it with the other performing arts as an independent unit instead of containing it within the realm of physical education. There has been greater emphasis upon performance and a considerable increase in the number of dance specialists and dance-related courses. The popularity of beginning technique classes has increased to such an extent that it often is difficult to get into a beginning class unless you enroll early. When enrolling, look at the dance course offerings. You might like to learn something about dance notation, dance production, anatomy for dancers, dance accompaniment, or dance history. These and other dance classes can introduce you to the fascinating world of dance.

A view of you

3

Before you take your first class, it is a good idea to take a good look at your dance equipment—your body instrument. The better the instrument, the faster you can expect to grow in your ability to perform. Your dance potential will be determined to some extent by your present physical condition, how well you have taken care of yourself in the past, and the body structure you have inherited.

Let each become all that he was created capable of being: expand, if possible, to his full growth; and show himself at length in his own shape and stature, be these what they may.

Richter
by Thomas Carlyle

You might like to list what you regard as your assets and your liabilities. You should at least mentally note those characteristics that you can improve not only to increase the quality of your dance experience, but also to improve each moment of your daily life. Your body is not something to be taken out of storage only occasionally; rather, it is your dwelling place for a lifetime.

Start your self-examination by an inspection of your general health habits. If you have followed a regimen of good nutrition and daily exercise and have gotten a sufficient amount of sleep each night, you are bound to enjoy a sense of physical well-being. If you have not, you may still feel good, but changing your bad habits to good ones is guaranteed to raise your efficiency level and supply you with more energy.

Are you aware of being overly tense much of the time? Do you become winded easily? Do you have difficulty maintaining your body balance? Do you lack energy or feel tired? Are your muscles flabby? Do you habitually slouch or slump? Are you overweight or underweight? These are some of the indicators of poor fitness. These also are conditions that you can improve if you have the desire and the willpower to do so.

Your approximately correct body weight can be determined by looking at the norms that have been established for your height, sex, and body type. Charts, such as the ones published by the Metropolitan Life Insurance Company, are available upon request at no cost. Your school health service and your personal physician will have this information. Your weight is considered acceptable if it is within 10 percent above or below the established norm.

In the average individual, 10 to 15 percent of the body weight is fat and about 40 percent is muscle. Muscles weigh more than fat but do not take up as much volume, which is the reason that individuals of the same height and weight may not have identical measurements. If your muscles are well developed and your body fat proportion is low, you will be likely to wear smaller clothing than do your friends whose muscles are undeveloped and whose fatty bulges are noticeable. Excessive fat impairs your ability to move because it gets in the way of movement, contributing to early fatigue and distorting the natural contours of the body. It also is psychologically destructive, particularly in our culture where "Fatty" is ridiculed. It is not quite so difficult to face the world if your friends call you "Skinny," but being too thin also lowers your physical fitness.

If you need to lose weight, consult your physician. Do it under professional guidance, and stay clear of diet fads even though some of your friends may urge you to follow their example and eat brown rice, endive, and bananas. You must meet your body's nutritional requirements but cut down your intake and increase the amount of exercise you do, which will help burn up stored body fat.

Does your body in general have good muscle tone? Are your muscles firm, smooth, and elastic? Good muscle tone is the result of proper diet and an adequate amount of exercise. Muscles can become flabby from too little exercise or hard and tense from overexercise. Neither is desirable.

How would you rate yourself in terms of motor ability? Can you perform common motor tasks easily and well? Are you fairly flexible? Are the muscles of your back, shoulders, abdomen, thighs, and arms strong? What about your endurance? Endurance can be measured by the length of time it takes after exercise for your heart rate to return to normal. The heart of an individual in top condition takes less time to return to normal than the heart of one who is not. During exercise the heart rate of a person who is physically fit will not increase as much as the rate of the person whose heart, lungs, and blood vessels are poorly developed due to insufficient daily activity.

How efficiently do you sit, stand, and walk? Do you know how to align the various parts of your body so that you can maintain your balance with a minimum of strain? Do you habitually have what is considered good posture? Do you extend your spine, lift your rib cage, and hold your abdomen in? Do you move with ease? There are mechanical principles that govern the way you use your body. These are based upon your physical structure, skeletal framework, and the actions of your joints and muscles as they relate to the force of gravity. Your body is a machine that is capable of turning out an incredible amount of work if you have learned how to operate it without wasting energy.

Finally, how would you characterize your general body type? Your potential for physical performance depends to a great extent upon the body build you have inherited. According to studies conducted by Dr. William Sheldon and associates at Columbia University,[1] individuals tend to fall into one of three general categories—ectomorphic, mesomorphic, or endomorphic. Most human bodies have some of the characteristics of all three general types, but they will tend to conform more nearly to the description of one of them. The ectomorph is extremely thin and frail, having small wrists, ankles, elbows, and knees, lacking in fatty tissue, and being of small dimension from front to back. The mesomorph has thick, heavy bones, large, firm muscles, and few fatty deposits and creates an overall impression of being strong and husky. The endomorph has the large bones of the mesomorph, but the musculature lacks tone, and there are excessive deposits of fat on the abdomen, hips, thighs, upper arms, and waist.

Because of your body build, you probably prefer to move in one way rather than in another. You tend to select kinds of movement you can perform successfully. Perhaps your body is designed for speed but not for endurance, or maybe you can do push-ups but not high leaps. Whatever your limitations, be assured that your range of movement will be extended as you realize what you are capable of being.

Care of Instrument

Rate yourself on the way in which you habitually care for your physical instrument. Use the following scale: 1 point, seldom; 2 points, usually; 3 points, always.

1. W. H. Sheldon, S. S. Stevens, and W. B. Tucker, *The Varieties of Human Physique* (New York: Harper and Brothers, 1940).

	Item	**Score**
1.	I eat a well-balanced diet.	_____
2.	I eat three meals a day.	_____
3.	I avoid snacking between meals.	_____
4.	I eat few sweets.	_____
5.	I sleep an average of eight to ten hours a night.	_____
6.	I relax several times during the day.	_____
7.	I avoid alcohol, drugs, and cigarettes.	_____
8.	I have few nervous habits and seldom worry.	_____
9.	I spend a part of each day in recreational activities.	_____
10.	I have an annual checkup with my physician.	_____
11.	I visit my dentist at least once a year.	_____
12.	I bathe, and brush and floss teeth daily.	_____
13.	I am well-groomed.	_____
14.	I generally feel good and have a lot of energy.	_____
15.	My weight is within ten percent of the norm for my height, sex, age, and body type.	_____

Total score _____

For men only

4

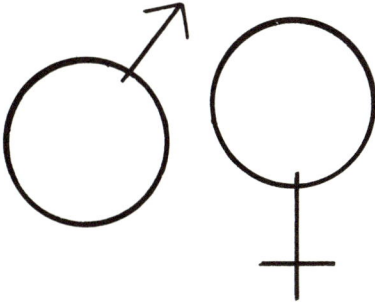

In these times of the Equal Rights Amendment and the Women's Liberation Movement, there is a tendency to overlook the fact that men, too, often are victims of unfair practices and policies. For instance, we traditionally maintain an attitude that certain tasks and professions are for women only; any man or boy expressing an interest in them becomes a target for negative criticism. We continue to embroider the word *Hers* upon such endeavors as nursing, homemaking, and being a beautician or secretary—and dancing, too. We even carry this attitude over into the realm of children's play. Traditionally, small boys have not played with dolls or engaged in pretend tea parties and have not been shown by their grandmothers how to knit. Few of them have ever been enrolled in a dance class. Yet we are legislating for the right of every individual to freedom of choice and equality of opportunity. If we truly believe that every man and woman is entitled to such equality, we must work to bring to an end the attitudes of prejudice that deter some individuals from pursuing fields that they are interested in.

Men always have and always will dance. As members of the human race, they derive satisfaction from moving rhythmically and from engaging in "body talk." Because of the structure of his body instrument, there are dance movements in which a man excels. Devoid of masculine partici-

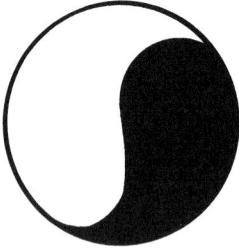

pation, dance would be incomplete in its communication and its commentaries upon life. Imagine *West Side Story* performed by an entirely female cast! Only when there are men and women dancing can the inherent meanings of dance be fulfilled. The completeness of an art so intimately related to human experience is realized only through combining the two elements, the Yin and Yang symbols of the Chinese, the masculine and the feminine.

Why, then, has there been a reluctance on the part of men students and instructors to participate in dance to the same extent as women? To some degree, men are active in recreational forms of dance in social and square dancing; they take part to a lesser degree in ethnic or folk dance; but in the contemporary art form of dance, modern dance, their numbers are tragically few. In all other forms of art this is not the case; indeed, a listing of the great artists throughout all of history reveals that men have made the most significant contributions to the world's culture. Names such as Michelangelo, Cézanne, Picasso, Wordsworth, Keats, Shelley, Sandburg, Wagner, Tchaikovsky, Beethoven, Bartók, Le Corbusier, Frank Lloyd Wright, and many others of similar stature come readily to mind. We cannot, however, compile a comparable list of great women artists. The number is astonishingly low.

The negative attitude toward men as participants in modern dance has been caused in part by circumstance and also by shortsighted administrative action. An artificial barrier was created by placing modern dance under the administration of women's physical education departments in a majority of colleges and universities and by appointing only women to the instructional staffs. Facilities for dance were located in the women's gymnasiums or placed on the distaff side of jointly shared physical education buildings. In many instances, modern dance became a part of the required program for women students, but seldom did it become incorporated in the men's required program.

Another factor contributing to the lack of participation by men has been the emphasis placed upon science in the structuring of school curricula. As a reaction to the technological accomplishment of the Russians in their launching of the historic Sputnik, because the implication of this first space vehicle threatened our sense of national security, American values suddenly became lopsided, and education quickly retooled itself in order to turn out future Einsteins, Edisons, Newtons, and Galileos.

Yet it is inconceivable that any great society could arise or survive without balancing its scientific with its artistic achievements. No *thinking* man would support a movement that has as its purpose the elimination of all art, literature, music, drama, and dance from the education and experience of an enlightened society; no *sensitive* man would elect to live in a world dedicated solely to the practical and the utilitarian, operated only by the machine and the computer. Realization of the important contribution art makes to humanity's total education prompted members of the American Association of School Administrators to pass a resolution during their 1959 convention that states in part:

> We believe in well-balanced school curriculum in which music, drama, painting, poetry, sculpture, architecture, and the like are included side by side with other subjects such as mathetmatics, history, and science. It is important that pupils, as a part of general education, learn to appreciate, to understand, to create, and to criticize with discrimination those products of the mind, the voice, the hand, and the body which give dignity to the person and exalt the spirit of man.

Experiences that broaden one's insights and instill deeper appreciation for the contribution art makes to the enrichment of living should not be denied any student, male or female.

The opportunity for men to take classes in modern dance is increasing. At present there is a slight trend toward transferring modern dance activities from women's physical education departments to schools of fine arts or to centers for the performing arts, where all classes are coeducational and are instructed by both men and women. Where dance still remains under the administration of women's physical education departments, more cocducational modern dance classes are being offered and also special classes limited to men only. Almost from the beginning, student dance organizations such as Orchesis and other modern dance clubs have encouraged men to participate as regular members. You should investigate the possibilities open to you on your campus.

One last point regarding dance for men should be discussed. It is a matter of deep concern to those who know of instances in which a male student, sincerely desirous of taking part in a modern dance class, has been discouraged from doing so because of a fear of being labeled a sissy. As was pointed out earlier in this chapter, masculinity is important and essential to the unity of the dance art. While some dance movements are performed equally well by both men and women, there are some that are essentially masculine, just as there are some that are essentially feminine. The dance instructor takes this into consideration in the planning of a lesson. The body structure of a man, with its high center of gravity, its strength, and its larger skeletal framework, enables him to move more vigorously, to cover wider distances in space, to leap higher into the air, and to expend a greater amount of energy than the female dancer. Ideas that are to be communicated through dance often demand a contrast between the masculine and the feminine. How else can some things be expressed? Some ideas can be expressed solely by male dancers—ideas having to do with heroes, warfare, imperial high potentates, and fathers and husbands. Women, on the other hand, also fill roles associated with their functions in society. They dance the lullabies, the Clytemnestras, and the feminine pursuits of spinning and weaving. Separately and together, they complement one another. At no time in history have men been excluded from dance; at one period, in fact, women were prohibited from participating in the ballet, and young boys, wearing wigs and skirts, replaced them. This no longer is the case, but this practice might have contributed to the false assumption, often held by those who are uninformed, that the male dancer is effeminate. Before you overlook what a class in modern dance might do for you, consider the following excerpt from statements issued by the members of the National Council on the Arts in Education at the conclusion of their 1963 national conference:

. . . not only is the potential scientist, engineer, businessman and statesman important to our national future, but also the emerging and performing artist. He must be recognized, stimulated and trained from the earliest age. A vital artistic culture, moreover, depends equally on the lover of art who judges with knowledge and taste . . . neglect of sensitively planned artistic education will not only lead to proliferation of mediocrity and vulgarity, but will head us on the way to Sparta.[1]

1. Reported in a paper presented by Finis E. Engleman, "Some Views on the Arts and American Education," at the 1963 National Conference on the Arts in Education.

The studio experience

5

Bind on thy sandals, O thou most fleet,
Over the splendour and speed of thy feet;

Atalanta in Calydon
by Swinburne

The dance studio is a laboratory, the place where you will perform experiments and learn to use your tools for dance. Its equipment is meager—a piano, possibly a few full-length mirrors, and a barre, a long, thin wooden pole horizontally attached to one or more walls. The most important aspects of the studio are its space, which is hopefully free of supporting structures such as posts or columns, and its floor, which is specially treated so you can glide upon its surface without slipping and having a smooth finish devoid of dangerous cracks or splinters.

Perhaps you will feel apprehensive as you enter the dance studio for the first time. This is a natural reaction that most of us experience at the beginning of any new venture. It does help to have a general idea of what is going to take place in the new situation and of what will be expected from you. There are things you can do to reduce those feelings of anxiety so you can begin your study of modern dance comfortably and with the expectation of exciting and adventurous times ahead.

In addition to making a self-assessment as recommended in chapter 3, another way of preparing yourself prior to entering class is to formulate an image of yourself as a dancer. This should not be too difficult, for all of us change roles constantly. We behave and feel one way when we are going out on a date, another way when visiting a sick friend or an elderly person, and still another when we join our friends for a day at the beach. We adapt ourselves to suit the occasion. Seeing yourself as a dancer might be a new role for you, but try doing it. Recall someone you know who moves well, and visualize yourself as having the same ability. Walk with ease into the studio, your body held high and proud and your arms relaxed, feeling self-assured and full of anticipation. Focus on the instructor for your next cue.

If you were not given instructions on what to wear for class at the time you enrolled in the course, find out what is required ahead of time by asking the instructor or someone who has taken the course before. You might be able to choose your attire, and if this is the case, you might have something in your own wardrobe that will do. In any event, what you wear should fit your body like a glove so that every movement can be seen. Leotards and tights are preferred for this reason. They permit freedom of movement without disguising the body's action. If you have the option, select a color that pleases you, one that gives you a "lift." Your feet will be bare to provide the best possible support for your body. Do not feel it is "square" for your body to look neat and orderly. It is efficient. Even if you think that long hair worn loosely is attractive in the ordinary classroom, it is unsuitable in the dance studio because it will get in your way. Anchor it with clips, an elastic band, hair spray, or a scarf, so that you will not be distracted.

Most dance instructors use a general plan such as the following one in their beginning modern dance classes:

First phase	— Techniques for a stationary base
Second phase	— Techniques and combinations for a moving base
Third phase	— Student experimentation
Fourth phase	— Presentation and evaluation

If the emphasis of the class is on the teaching of techniques only, the last two phases might be eliminated.

During the first phase, try to position yourself on the floor so you can see and hear the instructor without difficulty. Get as close to the source as you can for maximum benefit, instead of seeking the anonymity of the last row. You will be working in this place for a considerable portion of the lesson, standing, sitting, kneeling, and lying down as you exercise the muscles of your body. You will be given verbal instructions, often followed by a demonstration, so select an advantageous location.

It is highly beneficial for you as a beginner if the first techniques you learn are those that involve the large muscle groups. The starting position for any technique is important, so be sure you know where you are and how the various parts of your body should be placed before you begin the movement. Your entire body should be warmed up before attempting exercises that might otherwise cause strain. You will be bending, stretching, bouncing, and swinging large areas of your body to increase your circulation and to prepare you for more demanding actions. As you feel your muscles becoming warm, put more energy into the movement, increasing its range. But do not go beyond what your body can do with ease, for muscles only stretch when they are relaxed. Do not go all out until you are ready.

The lesson will progress from relatively simple techniques to more complex ones, but you will be ready at each step. There will be the challenge of moving in new ways, of starting to build your "dance vocabulary." Muscles that have been dormant for a long time will be called into play as you begin to discover the capabilities of your marvelous instrument. Again, be sure you understand the instructions, check the correctness of your starting position, and take it easy at first. You will begin to experience new sensations—you will begin to dance.

By the time you complete the first general phase of the lesson, you will be ready to move into the dancer's world, the world of space. You will be moving through it, crossing the floor in diagonal lines, going around the circumference of the studio, or breaking it up into a variety of geometric shapes. You will begin to become aware of how space is used and how similar it is to the painter's canvas. Your base of support will be constantly changing to carry you through the space. You will be given movement combinations based upon the movement principles you practiced in the first part of the lesson. Some might be very simple, such as a dance walk, but they are done with a quality and style that remove them from the realm of the ordinary. Something dancelike is imparted to even everyday movements, as you will see. You will become conscious of the visual effects and of the designs in space that result from various combinations.

As you move through space, you will be introduced to the various elements that give variety to movement combinations. Changes of rhythm, direction, level, or amount of applied force are some of the factors that result in change. The ability to use them is the craft of manipulation, the mark of the good choreographer.

When the class is given a new movement combination, you might attempt it first en masse, trying it out as a group as you cross the floor. On the other hand, you might be directed to perform it on your own, moving singly along a diagonal pathway from one corner of the studio to another. This is a time when the instructor can be of great help, for he can watch what each student is doing and make specific suggestions for improvement. When it is your turn, be ready to step out, and when it is not, watch your classmates, applying the suggestions they are given to your own efforts.

As you know, most dancing is accompanied by some kind of sound. In a performance, this could range from drumbeats to symphonic scores or from spoken words to electronic effects. In a dance class, however, the movements most often are accompanied by the piano. Do not be oblivious to it, for it is important to be able to relate what you do to the music. The accompaniment supports your efforts, making it easier and certainly more pleasant to perform. It gives you valuable clues such as when to start or stop, when to accent a rhythm, how fast or slow you should be going, and when the quality of the movement should be strong or weak. Learn to listen. Learn to be responsive to the sound.

You cannot experience dance totally unless there is a time during the lesson when you can work on your own. In some programs there may be special class offerings in improvisation or composition during which you learn to give form to the materials of dance, but a good teacher will find some time during the regular class session when you can begin to experiment, too. When you are given a problem to solve in your own way, you no longer will be an imitator. You will be free to be inventive and to apply some of the materials and principles you have worked with to something of your own. Instead of attempting to copy your instructor or that advanced student you admire, you will begin to find movements that belong to you—highly personal movements that lead to the discovery of your own uniqueness. Get to work immediately after the problem has been explained. Do not ponder too long; let your muscles do some of the thinking. There will be three parts to your solution: a beginning, a middle, and an ending. Try several solutions until your instincts tell you which is the best one. Hopefully there will be sufficient time left then to refine it and to repeat your pattern enough times until you have it memorized.

When there is an opportunity to have your work criticized, welcome it. This is the only way to measure the worth of what you have accomplished. You cannot view your study with perspective since you are inside it as you perform, even though you might have caught a glimpse of it if you did it in front of a mirror. The criticism you receive will be friendly and helpful, providing you with suggestions to consider if the work is to be revised and with ideas that could carry over to the next problem. There will not be many times when you will have the chance to show your solution to the entire class, but you might be asked to do it for a partner or for a small group. In turn, you will be asked to view what others have done, to help them improve the quality of their creative efforts. Dance has an honesty, an objectiveness when it is worked on together in this way. It is meant to be looked at in terms of its communication. If its meaning is unclear or its purpose does not come across, then the creator tries harder the next time, mindful of the pitfalls to be avoided.

Working with basic principles

6

At the root of the dance experience you will discover a number of natural laws of nature that you must deal with in order to acquire the skills that will enable you to use your body most effectively. As you understand and apply the principles involved in the production of all body movement, you will increase your ability to move efficiently and effectively, knowing what to expect from your body and how to direct it in order to attain the results you desire. These facets of nature are as unalterable and constant as the facts that the world is round and the sun rises and sets because it revolves upon its axis.

All these physical laws or principles operate together whenever your body is in motion, but in this chapter each will be considered separately for the sake of expediency and clarification. Following the discussion of each principle are a few suggestions of ways it can be applied to your own movements. As you try these ideas out, try to think of other ways in which you can illustrate the principle under consideration, too.

The first natural law to be dealt with is that of *gravity*. Gravity is the force that keeps us on the face of the earth instead of floating freely in the air. It exerts a constant downward pull upon our bodies along a vertical line, as if the earth's center were a magnet to which we are continually attracted. Any body position or movement other than remaining completely horizontal is an act against gravity. To defy it, we convert the fuel stored in our bodies into energy that is transmitted to our muscles. Using this energy, we can move in any direction, lift an arm or a leg, or leap or jump into the air. Inevitably, of course, we always return to earth since we cannot fly unassisted. As a person pushes against the ground in order to rise above it, he exerts energy. It is quickly diminished and cannot be replenished until he is again in contact with the ground. Learning to work with and against gravitational pull is a constant challenge to the dancer.

Experiment with the control of gravity

Stand upright, feet together, arms at sides. Lean forward slowly, keeping your body rigid. At the moment before the pull of gravity causes you to lose your balance, take a quick step forward to regain the upright body position. Repeat several times using this principle of fall and recovery.

Experiment with the control of gravity—Counterbalance

Again from the upright position with arms stretched overhead, begin leaning to one side. As soon as you sense that you are losing your balance, arch your upper body in the opposite direction, counterbalancing against the pull of gravity. Note that the more you counterbalance, the farther you can lean.

Let us next consider how movement is affected by *force*. As you know, your skeletal framework moves because of its layering of muscles that connect various parts of the framework together; when energized consciously or unconsciously, these muscles set the body in motion because of your intentional or unintentional application of energy to them through nerve impulses. Dance involves movements that you control consciously. Much of this control depends on the way in which you apply the force principle. You can produce variation in movements that otherwise would be the same by changing their amounts, speeds, and rhythms through the application of force. This is what gives dynamic shading to movement and varies its quality. When only a small amount of energy is applied to a movement, the effect produced will be one of weakness; a large amount of energy applied to the same movement will make it strong. If the force is applied evenly and smoothly, the dynamics of the movement will be different from those resulting from application of short, intermittent bursts of energy. Speed as well as duration of a movement depends in part upon the amount of force expended. The characteristics of specific dance qualities that are categorized as swinging, percussive, sustained, suspended, and collapsing are determined by the way in which the force principle is applied. The accompanying chart illustrates some of the possible combinations, each subject to further innumerable gradations.

Energy Factors Affecting Movement

Amount	Speed	Rhythm
weak	fast	irregular
weak	slow	irregular
weak	fast	constant
weak	slow	constant
moderate	fast	irregular
moderate	slow	irregular
moderate	fast	constant
moderate	slow	constant
strong	fast	irregular
strong	slow	irregular
strong	fast	constant
strong	slow	constant

Experiment with centrifugal force

Perform a series of turns in place. Increase your speed while relaxing both arms. Observe how your arms are inclined to move upward and outward; this is a manifestation of the effect of centrifugal force that causes movement to proceed out and away from its axis.

Experiment with force—Momentum

Place a small object on the floor and then move a considerable distance away from it. Run toward it as fast as you can, checking your speed at the last moment, so that you stop as close to the object as possible. Observe where and how you have to apply energy to overcome your forward momentum.

Modern dance also must deal with space, the area in and through which dance moves. Space itself is as neutral, as meaningless, and as empty as the canvas of a painter until through movement you transform it. Space is blank until it is filled with movement and broken up by lines of action.

As your body moves in a defined space, it gives shape and form to it. Space, at least all of it you intend to or can use, is defined by limitations that can be real or imaginary. Real space, such as that of the studio or a stage, is bounded by walls and ceilings, curtains, and proscenium arches. It is further delimited by standing objects such as pianos and tape recorders, chairs, tables, and members of the class, all of which take up room and limit the space in which you can dance. Imagined space is defined by self-imposed or teacher-imposed limitations that exist only in your mind. Through movement action and reaction you can convey the impression that you are confined within a small box, suspended within an inflated balloon, or constricted by an imaginary maze of solid walls and blind alleyways. Through your movement responses you can suggest that you are standing high on a hill or that you have fallen into a deep pit. Using your imagination, you can mold space into many forms and shapes. Its outer shell might be likened to a container encompassing a specific amount of space or volume. Within this volume your dance is enacted.

Experiment with sensing real space

Mark a small circle on the floor with tape or chalk. Stand in the center of the circle and close your eyes. With a series of small steps, move toward what you think is the edge of the circle. Now open your eyes to see how accurately you sensed the circle's outer limit. Practice this experiment until you successfully find the edge of the circle several times in a row. Repeat, using a wider circle.

Experiment with imagined space

Explore an imaginary cave, the dimensions of which become smaller and smaller as you penetrate its interior. Think about the way in which your movements change in order to accommodate to the lessened volume of contained space.

Time is concerned with the rate of speed and the rhythm we use to proceed from the beginning to the end of a movement, through a sequence of movements, or through a complete dance study or composition. Time has the property of progressing in a forward direction, of going ahead from one second to the next and from one minute to the next one. Dance, like music, consumes time and coexists with it. Dance never can be viewed or performed in its entirety within a given moment; it unfolds as time goes on, from its beginning to its ending.

The beginning dancer immediately must acquire the ability to be accurately "at one" with time—to be able to begin with the first beat of time, to identify its pulse and maintain step with it, and to sense its duration, its units, and its structure. Time, represented by the beating of a dance drum or the steady rhythmic accompaniment of the piano, sets the tempo for movement in beginning classes. It supports you and provides you with auditory signals for the tempo of your movements. You must learn to hear and respond to it. Listen to the pulse, the regularly recurring beat that moves steadily onward, not to the melody. You must be committed to it. You do not dance the melody; later on, you will design movement that will become its own melody in some ways.

After you have identified and responded to the pulsating beat of the music, you will begin to recognize *meter*, the small groupings of beats marked by regular (or sometimes irregular) accents. You will be able to recognize a waltz, a 3/4 meter, when you identify the accent that recurs on the first of every three beats. 123/123/123/123/. Meter varies; it can be 2/4, 4/4, 6/8, 5/8, or even mixed, so that you might have two measures of 2/4, then one of 6/8, and another of 5/4. It can become quite complex, demanding the utmost concentration. One established rhythm may have another superimposed upon it, and the two distinct rhythms may take place at the same time. Try clapping your hands in a 4/4 meter, accenting the first beat, while at the same time tapping your foot in a 3/4 meter. It is difficult to keep two separate meters going in the body, but it can be done. It is not quite so hard to perform to one meter while a partner uses another, or to move and maintain a meter against the one contained in the accompaniment. Counterrhythms, adding a new dimension to a steady, rhythmic beat, lend sophistication to rhythm and can be developed to a state of great complexity. They heighten the interest of a movement.

As soon as possible after you have mastered the response to imposed rhythm, you should begin creating your own. Avoid the too-regular and the pedestrian. *Pedestrian* implies ordinary walking, following a continuous *left, right, left, right, left right pattern*. It lacks interest. As Louis Horst used to tell his classes, if your idea *is* a pedestrian one, if your purpose *is* to be monotonous, use the one-two, one-two, one-two. But if this is the case, you do it intentionally, not because you cannot work in any other rhythm. You should become aware of the rhythmic element that pervades the world in which you live: the rhythm of the rain, of a skyline, of a heartbeat, and of the patterns of human emotions. Observe how your own rhythm of breathing changes, how it adjusts in response to differing conditions. When you are anxious or hurried, its rhythm is quick; when you are relaxed, as in deep sleep or when you are feeling contented, its rhythm becomes slow and even. Your resources for rhythm are contained in nature's almost limitless patterns. The more observant you are of nature's variety, the more selective you will be in choosing the rhythms best suited to the content of your choreography.

Experiment with time—Duration

Try this experiment with a group of friends. Use a watch with a second hand. Ask your friends, beginning on the signal "go," to count sixty seconds to themselves and to clap their hands when they think the minute is up. Observe the variation in their responses. You can check your own time duration sense in a similar fashion by looking away from the watch until you feel that a minute has expired.

Experiment with time—Accent

Select the title or first line of a popular song. Notice which syllables are stressed or accented. Tap the rhythm of the accents with your finger several times. Now use this rhythm to compose a movement pattern.

Dance movements also are limited by the *structure* of the human body and by the manner in which its movable parts are connected. The points of connection are the joints, such as the knee, elbow, hip, and shoulder. How a segment of the body can move is determined by which one of four types of joints connects it to its adjacent segments. Each type is capable of producing a specific action; the hinge, pivot, ball-and-socket, and ovoid joints all perform differently. The hinge permits a bending and straightening action like that produced at the knee, ankle, and elbow. The pivot allows turning or partial rotation such as movements of the head, for instance. The ball-and-socket joints, like the ones located at the shoulder and the hip, enable the arms and legs to rotate. The ovoid, such as those joints that connect the fingers to the palm of the hand, allow movement in an oval direction.

You might have observed that although the foot is connected to the leg bone by a hinge-type joint, which should limit the joint only to flexion and extension, it nevertheless can be rotated and turned inward and outward. This is because of the way in which the many small bones of the foot itself are jointed together. The spine, too, has the capacity to move because of the slippage that can take place between its vertebrae, although it is not connected by true joints. It can bend forward, backward, and sideward; it can twist and ripple because of the nature of its structure.

Experiment with structure—Hinges

Using at least five different parts of the body in a sequence, compose a movement pattern limited to hinge action.

Experiment with structure—Body segments

Beginning with a movement of your head and letting the movement travel downward to your feet, employ in sequence the following body segments: head, shoulders, rib cage, waist, hips, knees, and ankles.

Finally, and most importantly, dance movement is flavored by something Delsarte stated as the law of the personality in his analysis of the nine laws of gesture. Something of your nature, your individuality, and your temperament are imparted to your movements. Even when you imitate the motions of others, you cannot help reflecting a bit of yourself. This reflection is uniquely significant and revealing. It imparts freshness and subtle shading to all movement, preventing it from becoming purely mechanical. This is in part why dance is art, not exercise.

> *Wonder is not precisely knowing,*
> *And not precisely knowing not,*
> *A beautiful but bleak condition.*
>
> Wonder is not precisely knowing
> by Emily Dickinson

In summary, then, dance is subservient to certain principles and natural restrictions. It is governed by the laws of gravity and energy, and it can change dynamically as the elements of force, speed, and rhythm are controlled. Its designs are created by molding and shaping the space in which it exists. In addition, the dancer's capabilities are limited by the structure of his or her skeletal framework, and energy supplied through the nervous system which is transmitted to the musculature. All of these factors combine in ways unique to the individual.

Techniques

7

It should be pointed out that dance techniques in and of themselves are useful merely for the purpose of developing skills and providing the dancer with a vocabulary of dance movements. Techniques deal with craftsmanship. They are a means by which you become better able to use your body instrument, and should not be confused with the final art product, the dance composition. Techniques lack meaning; they are imitative, repetitious, usually of short duration, and incorporate only one or two principles of design. A dancer never ceases working upon his technique, just as a pianist never stops performing exercises at the keyboard, but a perfect *grand plié*, a split fall, or the most spectacular stag leap are but preparations for artistic and communicative experience.

Learning techniques will help you acquire good working habits. You practice extending your foot each time you lift your leg until this becomes a habit. You learn to flex your knees and ankles as you land from a jump so that ultimately you will be able to perform a series of jumps without strain and without fatigue. You acquire a consciousness of good body line and begin to sense the relationship of one body segment to another and to the totality of movement. You experience the flow of a movement that is initiated by one part of the body and spreads throughout the rest of the body. You acquire a movement vocabulary that you will use and vary as you construct combinations, phrases, and, later on, as you compose dance studies and full-length compositions. You increase the capabilities of your body instrument and extend its range by means of carefully planned exercises that increase balance and control, lengthen muscle groups, and contribute to your increased strength, flexibility, and efficiency. You become better able to direct your physical energy and to conserve your forces as you gain skill and better understand the way in which your body and its moving parts function. You learn to make greater demands upon your instrument and to achieve them with clarity. You become confident of your ability to move—to move well.

When a new technique is presented, there should be an opportunity to experiment with it. After you have had a chance to practice it—to perfect it to some degree under the supervision of your dance instructor—you should then begin to use it in your own way. The application of some of the basic principles, discussed in the previous chapter, to any new technique will change it and make it more useful to you. Any technique is altered when its rhythm, direction, speed, or spatial design are changed; when it is transferred from one part of the body to another; when its order (sequence) is reversed; when its range is extended or shortened; or when its level or its focus is relocated. If there is not sufficient time during the class session for you to explore some of the possibilities inherent in a new technique, find some opportunity on your own, preferably immediately following your class while the experience is fresh in your mind and body.

Keep a notebook, listing each technique as it is presented in class, for it is not customary for an instructor to follow a textbook as you are introduced to new techniques and concepts. If you make some sort of a record of each technique, you will not have to rely upon memory as you practice outside of class. There is a system for notating movement, Labanotation, but to use it requires extensive study. For your purposes, simply jot down a few verbal descriptions and use stick figures to illustrate the positions of the body.

It really is essential that you practice your techniques on a daily basis. You should reinforce what you are given in a class that meets only two or three times a week if you expect to improve to any extent.

Technique classes generally begin with exercises known as warm-ups. These involve the large muscle groups of the thighs, spine, abdomen, and shoulders. They stimulate circulation of the blood to those parts of the body that might otherwise be insufficiently activated to meet the further demands that are to be made of them, and they also increase the flexibility of your body instrument. Warming up minimizes mishaps such as sprains

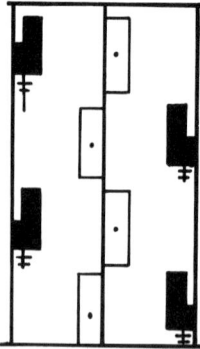

A prance in Labanotation

and strains that might cause serious injury. It also prevents undue muscular soreness. Particular attention usually is directed toward warming up the muscles of the legs and feet since these support the weight of your body and carry you through space as you move across the dance studio.

Begin your warm-ups gradually. As you feel your muscles lengthening and the body segments loosening at the joints, begin to increase the amount of force you apply to the movement. You are the best judge of how far to go and how long to continue. No two bodies have the same capabilities, for no two are exactly alike. Individuals of one general body type have movement problems and capabilities that differ considerably from those belonging to another classification. The short, somewhat stubby body with short extremities frequently will be very flexible, while the "string bean" variety will not. On the other hand, the tall, thin individual often can get higher into the air. In any case, you are not competing with anyone else. You might not be able to bounce forward and reach beyond your toes while keeping your knees extended as well as your nearest classmate, but you can increase your own range if you are willing to work at it. You can bring your body to a full realization of its own potential.

After approximately ten minutes of warm-ups, you will be ready to learn new and more challenging techniques and to review those you learned during earlier class periods. Sometimes the entire remaining part of the lesson will be based on a single technique, or a principle of movement such as quality or dynamics, or an aspect of design such as the use of contrasts or levels. The format for your class sessions will change from time to time as the instructor becomes aware of your needs. No two classes ever are exactly alike, for each is composed of a different set of individuals. In most class sessions, a new technique or combination will be analyzed and often demonstrated for you so you can see how it should be performed. Then you will have an opportunity to try it, to repeat it many times, and to receive suggestions and make corrections as they are needed. Listen carefully to the analysis; become aware of how you are moving and consciously direct your instrument; develop a sense of the total involvement of all parts of your body even though the action is concentrated in one specific area. As you wait your turn to cross the floor during a practice period, observe what your classmates are doing, and try to analyze their difficulties. In this way you will be able to better analyze your own.

There are certain fundamental practices that will help you perform every dance technique well. Being *centered* is of utmost importance, for only then are you ready to move out in any direction quickly and accurately. Consciously assemble your entire body so that it is under your complete control *before* you begin to move. Being centered implies more than placing your body in a completely balanced position; it means coming into focus, concentrating on total integration of the self, physically and mentally. You must find the exact center point of your personal universe and sense your authority there; with full confidence you must locate yourself at the core of your unique oneness, with every part of you alert for the first movement. Being centered does not mean necessarily that you stand at attention. You can be centered in any preliminary position—standing, sitting, lying prone, or kneeling. It means being assembled, being vitally aware, and being ready with everything under complete control.

Placement is another important condition that will affect your technical performance. Each segment of the body must be aligned with another in order to produce a visual unity that is pleasing and at the same time efficient. Placement can be either static or dynamic. If the body is motionless, then *static* placement is involved. When it moves, its placement is constantly adjusted; this is *dynamic* placement. The body segments, like building blocks, balance upon each other. To achieve balance, you must make constant adjustments since, as you know, your body is subject to the law of gravitational pull. If one segment is shifted from the vertical line of balance, another must be moved in the opposite direction in order to maintain that balance.

Aesthetically, some positions are interesting and others are not. It is possible to attain balance without achieving the desired visual objective. If, for example, you were to curve your spine by bending forward, while at the same time releasing your pelvis so that the curved line of the back would be broken, the visual results would not be pleasing. If the body tilts backward instead of forward when you perform a series of horizontal leaps in a forward direction, the cause is poor placement. Not only is the efficiency of the movement impaired, but the thrust of the line of action is diminished. Good placement is positioning your body effectively, taking efficient functioning and visual line into account. As you perform each technique, you should concentrate upon this relationship of the parts to the whole.

Control of *breathing* also will assist you in moving well and efficiently. Any opening gesture or lifted movement, when accompanied by an inhalation of breath, will become fuller and more enriched. Breathing gives tremendous support to movement. You should control it and become aware of how to use it to your advantage. Frequently its rhythm during dancing will be different than that of normal breathing, since it will be determined by the particular movement combination you are doing. Its ebb and flow is more likely to be uneven than even. When the movement is to collapse or be drawn inward, the breath should be expelled. All this action should take place in the diaphragm, not in the chest. To illustrate this, center your body in a standing position, rise to your toes (relevé) while lifting both arms sideward and upward, and at the same time inhale deeply. Now repeat this rising motion, but exhale instead of inhaling. How do the two ways of breathing affect your performance? To illustrate the rhythmic control you must have over your breathing, try this combination. Stand in first position and quickly collapse your torso to the right side on count one. Slowly return to your starting position on counts two, three, four, and five. Exhale as you collapse and inhale as you recover. Repeat to the other side. Your breath rhythm should be 12345/12345. Exhale on the count of one. With each technique you learn, discover the breathing pattern that will give it the best support.

Each dance technique should be performed meticulously. If the technique is one in which the movement is concentrated in one part of the body, you still must relate other parts to it. If it is a technique involving the feet and legs, you must be aware of the way in which it relates to the spine, shoulders, arms, and head. With most techniques, some parts of the body will move while other parts will be fixed. Be conscious of both aspects. Learn to feel the technique, sensing the way the muscles function and what lines are produced as a result of the action. While the beginning and the ending of a technique are important, the path in between is of even more concern. Become aware of the interplay of the parts of the action.

In addition to developing an inner awareness, a kinesthetic response to a technique, observe it externally. Mirrors are provided for this in the dance studio. Use them whenever you have the opportunity. Let your eyes assist you in making corrections and adjustments. Compare what you see in the mirror with the model that was set for you by the demonstration. Your techniques will improve only as you practice them, but be sure *before* you practice that you understand exactly what to do and how to do it. Your experience should include external observation as well as development of internal awareness.

Technique classes are stimulating and enjoyable. There, you receive specific directions and learn to follow them. Your instructor assists you in perfecting patterns of movement by analyzing your difficulties and suggesting means by which you can correct them. You learn to control your body and to be able to direct its actions as you build a technical vocabulary. As you improve, you will gain a sense of accomplishment, for you will be able to observe your own progress. As you eventually are able to perform a deep *plié* with perfect balance and correct placement or a series of crystal clear prances with perfect precision, you will experience satisfaction. Each success will contribute to the strength of your self-image. As you learn the craft of modern dance, you will be better able to speak the language of dance. Technical skill is the foundation for dance communication. It is the means leading to this end.

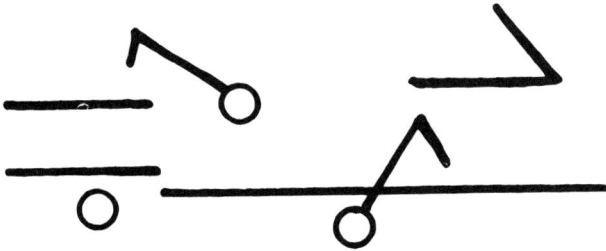

Eighteenth-Century
Dance Notation

Stretch your imagination

8

There was a child went forth everyday,
And the first object he look'd upon,
That object he became.

by Emily Dickinson

Imagination—what is it? One definition describes it as the picturing process of the mind, the ability all of us have to construct images from the memory of an experience. It is the secret weapon of poets, painters, composers and inventors—of all who work creatively. No one lacks an imagination, but not everyone uses his often enough. We become trapped by the real and the practical.

Imagination becomes strengthened through use. One way to exercise it is to use the process of improvisation, the theme of this chapter. Most dancers will agree that this is the most rewarding and delightful part of their dance training, for there are no restrictions, limitations, concerns about technique, or rigid forms to be adhered to. When you improvise, you are free to follow your own instincts and inclinations without having to wonder how something might look. You do it for yourself, not for an audience.

When you improvise, you do not need a dance teacher or a studio. In fact, you probably will do better without them in some place of privacy. Play with suggestions. Strive for the absurd and the ridiculous. Have you ever made faces in front of a mirror? Think of your body as a face, capable of making all kinds of weird and strange expressions. For a start, try some of the illustrations and suggestions that follow. Later, as you get in the habit of improvising, you can find your own (probably better) stimuli. They are plentiful, both externally in your environment and internally in your memory.

Let your movements be dancelike; let them flow together as you connect them, one movement giving rise to another. Avoid making literal gestures. You are dancing, not acting. The roots of movement might be contained in natural gestures, but you should transform them. Make rhythmic changes, energy changes, and tempo changes. Try transferring a gesture to another part of the body.

Illustration: Yawn several times deep and fully. Notice how it feels, how your mouth stretches and your chest expands and contracts, and how deeply you inhale. Now attempt to duplicate the action with one hand. Make it yawn, duplicating the original act as well as you can. Try yawning with both arms as the focal point, but move your entire body in response. You can do the same thing using both legs, one arm and one leg, your spine, or any other movable body part. Try a continual series of yawns, each one with a different part of your body.

Other suggestions for transfers:

A wink
A smile
A giggle
A good-bye wave
An embrace
Chewing and swallowing
A sneeze

Objects having a characteristic shape and way of moving are fun to improvise. As you try to become the object, you will forget yourself in the absorbtion of moving in strange ways. Make the sky the limit as you explore the absurd and the improbable. Perhaps, as you work, a dramatic situation will develop. Let it lead you further as you improvise.

Illustration: Be an umbrella and discover ways of opening and shutting yourself. Indicate your shape and texture. Maybe you have a broken rib, or you stick as you are opened, or you turn inside out on a windy day. Use your imagination.

Other suggestions of things to become:

A refrigerator
A window shade
A sewing machine
A balloon
A mixer
A vacuum cleaner
A merry-go-round
An elevator

Sounds as well as visual stimuli can provide you with starting points for improvisation. Music has set feet dancing since the beginning of time. Any sound can do the same thing. Your movements should bear a relationship to what you hear—they should be full and round, thin and intermittent, rhythmically monotonous, rising and falling, strong or weak, depending on what best describes the characteristics of the sound.

Illustration: From a sitting position, follow the rise and fall of a police siren, using any part of your body. Experiment with other movable parts. Combine a number of them. On a moving base travel through space, your entire body rising and falling as it goes along. Add dynamics to the movement, changing its intensity. Make it appear to be coming from a distance, gradually increasing its volume as it comes nearer.

Suggestions for working with sounds:

A dripping faucet
Ice in a glass
The five o'clock whistle
A purring cat
A squeaky shoe
A barking dog
A snoring man
The rattle and rustle of a newspaper

When you have become accustomed to treating the literal in a non-literal way and you are confident that you are dancing your improvisations, not acting them out, try dealing with human subjects whose occupations have specific characteristics you can recall. Even if you find it easier to start your improvisations with movements that are closely related to the actual, search for points of departure. Make illogical changes. Let your thoughts jump around and your movements change correspondingly.

Illustration: Become a bird-watcher. From behind a blind, sight a rare species. Observe the bird through a pair of binoculars. Become the binoculars, the bird, or a wing or beak. Let your mind leap from one aspect of bird-watching to another.

Other suggested occupations:

A juggler
A bandleader
A seamstress or tailor
A butterfly collector
A magician
A pastry cook

Undoubtedly you have noticed the effect of moods upon physical behavior and how changes in the way we feel are revealed by our posture, movement responses, and even our rhythm. When you improvise with a mood, make it larger or smaller than life-size. Exaggerate the actions of the body. Use less or more energy than the normal state would require. Reveal the mood with all parts of the body, sometimes as an isolated movement and sometimes with all parts participating. As you improvise with a mood, you may find that it deepens. This is because your feelings begin to accompany what you are doing and are affected by the motions you are making. This is a two-way street: emotion results in motion, and motion can produce emotion. Some people go for brisk walks or dig in the garden when they are feeling depressed. The activity has a therapeutic value for them and replaces that low mood with something more positive. Before you improvise with a mood, take a moment to really feel it.

Illustration: Begin from a wide base such as a lunge or a second position. The mood to be expressed is aggression. Make forceful gestures. Strike, pound, kick, and shove with your fists, feet, head, elbows, and shoulders. Take a few strong, purposeful steps and attack something. Twist, tear, and whip it. Carry it to the point of destruction.

Suggestions for moods to get into:

> Frustration
> Curiosity
> Timidity
> Anticipation
> Anxiety
> Meditation
> Weariness
> Sullenness
> Foolishness

Practically anything can be a source for improvisation. What you see, hear, touch, feel, and even taste can be the stimulus. And your memory is a veritable treasure chest for you to explore. As you sensitize yourself to react and respond, you will release the creative forces that slumber within you. The walls of your inhibitions will come tumbling down as your imagination soars, and up you will grow!

On being creative

9

The nature of creativity is not yet fully understood. As a subject, it holds continued fascination for philosophers, psychologists, educators, geneticists, critics, aesthetes, and those immediately concerned with creativeness, the artists themselves. We can recognize manifestations of creativity, as in a final work of art, but no acceptable answers have been found to satisfactorily explain why it happens. Are we born with creative talent, or does it occur because of the environment in which we are placed? If your father was a composer of music, will it be within your nature to become one also? Would we have the urge to create art if our frustrations, our aggressions, or our sexual drives and needs were satisfied? Are artistic endeavors merely sublimations or the rechanneling of energies? Is there such a thing as an artistic personality in contrast to a scientific one? If the entire educative process were to be focused upon the goal of creativity, would there be a modern Renaissance? Is there really anything that is new, or is it merely that someone has discovered a different way of arranging the already known? Is creativity due to a combination of genes? Is it accidental? Are some more innately endowed than others, or do we have equal potentials? Will creativity flower in spite of adversity, or because the climate is especially favorable?

We have few facts upon which to base any valid conclusions. We can find arguments to support each point of view, but at best these only can be philosophical and speculative. As investigations continue, someday we may better understand creativity.

For the purpose of discussing the creative as it pertains to modern dance, let us proceed from the premise that every individual, every man or woman, everyone who has ever existed or will be born—past, present, or

What Do You See?

future—is *divinely unique.* Let us also assume that each person is capable of placing the imprint of his uniqueness upon that which he creates and, as a result, is incapable of producing an exact replica of the work of another.

When a student of dance first learns that he is expected to be creative, he sometimes entertains certain misgivings about his ability to meet this challenge. If you imagine that you are going to be expected to compose an entire dance or even a section of one before you have the tools with which to do this, allay your fears. Your first use of movement in an inventive way will be based upon only what you have learned about dance movement. In essence, you will use the problem-solving method, applying your knowledge to the solution of a simple problem. You will not be expected to create from a vacuum. In the beginning, you will not be asked to listen to some music and then be requested to compose a dance to it. Before you conduct any experiment, you will be given some tools to assist you. You will acquire a vocabulary of movement through learning some of the basic techniques; you will be given an analysis of rhythm and will have had many opportunities to work rhythmically; you will learn how to produce movement quality by the application of force in different ways; you will become aware of how to use space, levels, and focus to direct movement; and your body will be given preparation and practice so that it can respond to your direction.

In your first assigned problems you will be expected to carry out a few simple instructions. For example, you might be asked to move two parts of your body instrument together until they touch, such as your right hand to your left knee or your right foot to your left elbow. First, you might do this slowly and then slowly return to your starting position; or you might do it quickly, or combine the slow and fast, or alternate from one side to the other. You might be given a problem in which you are to compress your body, folding it up until it occupies the smallest possible space and then expanding it until it fills the maximum amount of space that is possible. You might be

What Do You See?

asked to combine several movements you have learned, such as a triplet, a side leg lift, a body twist, and a turn, and to perform these in several different orders or at different speeds. You might be asked to use your imagination to vary the dance walk. Try walking on hot coals, cool grass, or thin ice. You might be given an assignment in which you have the fun of dealing with the absurd—move as an egg being fried in a hot skillet, as an umbrella on a windy day, as a broken record, or as a hungry mouse-trap. You might be handed an object—a piece of frayed rope, a small pebble, a scrap of cloth—and be asked to react to it in some way. You should relate to it in your own way. You are not searching for right or wrong answers. As long as you observe the limitations of the problem, you are right. Each problem will be solved in a different way because of the uniqueness of person that we have discussed. This is not to say that your first solution necessarily will be your best, for almost inevitably there will be ways to improve what you have done, but each problem you deal with will increase your capacity for handling more difficult ones until at last you are able to meet the challenge of the full-length composition.

Sometimes your problems will be of such a nature that you will work as an individual as you search for a solution. Other times, you might work with a partner or be assigned to a small group. In these instances, the solutions represent joint thinking and planning. Working with others demands certain things that are unnecessary when we work as individuals. First, the responsibility should be shared. There should be a balance between suggesting ideas and accepting those of others. If you customarily assume the leader's role, the group probably will recognize this and go along with you. In this instance, however, try not to dominate to the extent that others have no opportunity to make suggestions. On the other hand, you habitually may depend on others for leadership. Remember, you have the responsibility of contributing to the group. Offer suggestions and hold up your end of the load. The dynamics of the group process fluctuate for each member of the group during the time of the exploration. Each individual should be able to accept the suggestions of others and to contribute good ones of his own.

Working creatively is working constructively and harmoniously. If you have to discard some part of what you have composed in order to refine the whole, do so willingly. It is a temptation to hold on to something you have spent much time and effort on or to dismiss the whole because a small part went wrong. Sometimes you can build only after you have laid waste; from the ashes of the old will arise the new. The rhythm of progress is erratic, similar to the organic process in nature. The seed may germinate slowly, or it suddenly may burst open; the succeeding steps of the growth process may be steadily progressive or occur in spurts; the final unfolding might be dramatically sudden or subtly almost imperceptible. The most important thing is to stay with the problem from beginning to end. How you deal with it is a measure of your Self, for as Yeats has written, "the test of one's harmony is one's power to absorb the heterogeneous and make it harmonious."

Modern dance, perceptively and sensitively taught, will encourage the release of your creative powers. You are to do more than imitate your instructor or use your body instrument merely as a technical display. Modern dance employs a meaningful educational methodology that emphasizes individual application of knowledge to problem solving. A high premium is placed upon your efforts to bring forth something from your own "still center." You will be encouraged to originate, not imitate, and to reveal, not conceal, your uniqueness as the one original of your kind. As you are given opportunities to explore with movement you are led in the direction of dance communication. As you become articulate in dance, you will be able to express the quality of your thinking. The ultimate is learning to dance your Self.

What do we know about creativity? What investigations have been made? Some advances in our understanding about the creative process have taken place, and many investigations currently are under way. For example, we now know more about some of the characteristics that are commonly shared by successful artists as revealed by a recent study conducted by the Institute of Personality Assessment and Research at the University of California. One important characteristic is the ability to think in terms of concepts—to be able to formulate abstract ideas that are independent of concrete existences and go beyond that which is factual. The American Institute for Research and the University of Pittsburgh are cooperating in project TALENT, a long-range study that is concerned with the identification, development, and utilization of human talents. Already they have developed a reliable instrument for assessing creativity, the Talent Creativity Test. This test is designed to measure an individual's ability to find ingenious solutions to practical problems. Note the emphasis upon problem solving and the high acceptability of solutions that are ingenious.

In conferences such as those held annually by the National Council on the Arts in Education, the problems of creativity and finding ways in which we can foster and promote the artistic side of our culture through education are emphasized and discussed. Federal support for the performing arts, as well as grants to support research in the arts has become actuality. At no other time in American history have the arts been given such wide recognition and support.

Through your dance classes, you will be given some of the keys that can open the doors of your creativity. You also can supply some for yourself. Here are some ways in which you can exercise your creative abilities.

First of all, *be curious*. Ask questions of yourself and of others. Pretending to know about all things is disguise for ignorance and so, frequently, is silence. Real knowledge is obtained by asking *why* and *how*.

Avoid imitation, at least in the structure of your thinking. It is natural to feel more comfortable in following the current styles of dress and patterns of behavior, but to accept common thinking and prejudice and to buy what you hear and read without first reasoning out your action is nothing short of blind ignorance.

Challenge the status quo. This advice is not intended to encourage the performance of ridiculous acts of protest—then it could be destructive. However, you must be constantly aware of the changes that are taking place as investigations and discoveries bring new insights that clarify man's thinking. Civilization does not stand still; it is one thing today and another tomorrow. You, yourself, change from day to day. Be sensitive to trends and look for the signs that indicate change. Sometimes you should search for them in unlikely places. Turn off the thruway and make a few excursions down side roads.

Investigate the noncredit aspect of your campus. Go to a concert; visit the art gallery and museums; find time to do a bit of browsing in the library instead of using that facility only for preparation of an assignment; drop in for an informal chat with one of your teachers; join a camera club; see a play or a dance concert; try out for a campus musical show. These are important plus values of a high school or college education.

As a final suggestion, spend some of your waking time *dreaming*. There is a time to be alone with one's thoughts. Give your imagination some free rein and let it lead you where it will. You will come closer to knowing yourself if you do this—closer to the realization of the universal goal, the harmony of the inner and outer Self.

All in all, try to avoid clichés in movement, in your ways of thinking, and in your patterns of speech. All of us are guilty of using them and of imitating others or falling back on that which has been used so frequently that it has become trite. But when we do so, we are denying the existence of our own individuality. It is far easier to be imitative; it takes much less effort than to search for new ways of expression, but it certainly is less rewarding and less satisfying. Exercise your originality whenever you can, for just as you can strengthen your muscles by exercise, you also can strengthen and increase your ability to be original if you exercise your creativity. Train yourself to look beyond the obvious and to discover the unique. Try the exercises at the end of this chapter, designed to stimulate your ability to invent new images with words and with movement.

Through your dance experiences you will be able to understand all art and artists better. As Robert Henri has written on the subject:

Art, when really understood, is the province of every human being. It is simply a question of doing things, anything, well. It is not an outside, extra thing. When the artist is alive in any person, whatever his kind of work may be, he becomes an inventing, searching, daring, self-expressing creature. He becomes interesting to other people. He disturbs, upsets, enlightens, and he opens ways for better understanding. Where those who are not artists are trying to close the book, he opens it, shows there are still more pages possible. The world would stagnate without him and the world would be beautiful with him; for he is interesting to himself and he is interesting to others.[1]

WORD IMAGES

To enhance and strengthen the images evoked by words, we often resort to the use of similes. Unfortunately, their effectiveness is diminished through overuse. Try to fill in the blanks with fresh descriptive words to substitute for those in common use.

Free as a _____   Fat as a _____

Hard as a _____   Sharp as a _____

Straight as a _____   Hungry as a _____

Thin as a _____   High as a _____

Old as the _____   Wrinkled as a _____

Crazy as a _____   Dry as a _____

1. Robert Henri, *The Art Spirit* (Philadelphia: J. B. Lippincott Co., 1960), p. 15.

Weak as a _____   Mad as a _____

Red as a _____

Words to be avoided: *bird, rock, arrow* or *pin, rail* or *pencil, hills, loon, kitten, beet, pig, razor* or *knife* or *tack, bear, kite, prune, bone, hornet* or *hatter.*

MOVEMENT IMAGES

Through the use of images, the formation of mental pictures, your body can assume various shapes, and the quality of its motion can be guided toward meaningful dance gesture. Try some of the following, noting your responses.

1. Point your ears like a fox.
2. Point your foot like a sharpened pencil.
3. Insert an extra vertabra at the base of your neck.
4. Think of your spine as a Greek column.
5. Zip up your jacket.
6. Roll your head like a marble.
7. Bounce a ball inside your torso.
8. Ripple your arm like a flag.
9. Sink to the floor like water draining from a tub.
10. Open and close your legs like a pair of scissors.
11. Jump up and down on coiled wire springs.
12. Move around inside a low-ceilinged cave.
13. Be an accordion.
14. Be bacon crisping in a hot skillet.
15. Be a goldfish in a bowl.

Movement by design

10

Design is the purposeful way in which the elements of an art form are combined. It is a plan for organizing the materials of the craft. To design a painting, a piece of sculpture, a building, or a dance phrase is to plan the use of the materials in such a way that ideas and concepts are brought into meaningful focus. It is design that shapes and forms an art. It is the logical arrangement of various parts that produces a satisfying whole. Design rather than improvisation is what gives rise to composition.

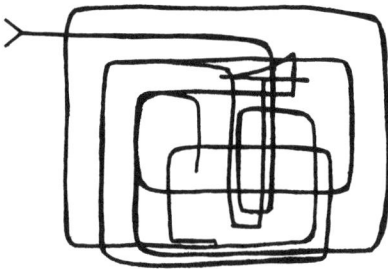

Approximate Floor Plan for Graham's Opening Dance

Design applied to modern dance is a visual affair; it is what meets the eye of the observer. This poses a critical problem for the dancer, for although he must be within the dance experience, he nevertheless must be aware of the visual impact of his movements and of his effect upon the watcher. If this is disregarded, dance is reduced to improvisation or personal therapy. In a sense, the dancer is a performer and a spectator at the same time. The dancer must not only "feel" the movement but in the same instant regard it from a distance with the eye of the discerning critic.

Being aware of design should become a working habit from the beginning of your dance experience. Even when you are building a vocabulary of movement or are practicing a new technique, you should ask yourself,

"How does this look?" How does your body instrument in motion compare with the instruments of the others in the class and with the original demonstration? What adjustments are necessary to make it visually correct? How can its design be changed to give it more interest and more meaning?

Although as you work with the element of design you hopefully will consider it in its entirety, for our purpose in this discussion it is separated into four categories: linear design, contained design, temporal design, and structural design. Although we shall examine each aspect singly, you should recognize that they operate collectively.

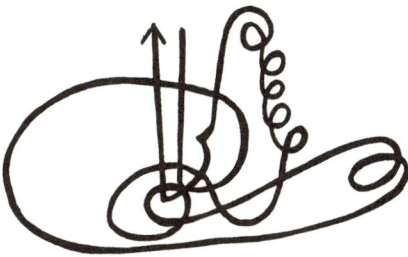

Approximate Floor Plan for
Wigman's Hexentanz

The *linear* aspect of dance design is concerned with the shifting patterns made by the motion of the body, by the outlines that are established between the various segments of the body instrument, and by the way in which the dance space is carved into numerous geometric shapes. Unless the body is completely static and motionless at a point of arrest, these linear patterns will change constantly, continuously forming, dissolving, and reforming. Angles, curves, and lines that are straight or broken are perceived when relationships are established between arm and torso, head and shoulder, or foot and leg. Consider, for example, the difference between the linear design when the foot is pointed and when it is flexed or when an arm is held away from the body and when it is resting against it. Each combination produces a unique shape that the eye can perceive. The ability to deal with the relationships that are established between all parts of the body contributes to the interest and clarity of your movements. The critic refers to this ability when he pays tribute by stating, "This dancer has a fine line." Ballet dancers seem to develop this awareness earlier than modern dancers, perhaps because ballet instruction traditionally has placed such emphasis upon line. However, it is equally important for the modern dancer to develop it.

The linear shaping of the dance space involves the shapes that are formed as the dancer moves through space. The simplest illustration is what is referred to as the *floor pattern*. This design evolves as the dancer travels through space, moving from point to point. If you observe a painter as he moves his brush across the surface of his canvas and breaks up the surface by drawing lines upon it, you might see how this to a degree parallels the method the dancer uses to produce a floor pattern. If the floor surface is thought of as the canvas and the dancer's feet as the brush, the completed design would look like the linear aspect of a painting. However, since the dancer's feet leave no permanent imprint on the surface, all dance design passes into memory. You can and should, however, work from the reality of a permanent design.

Consider first the total area in which you are to move. You might draw its boundaries on a piece of paper or the chalkboard. Then decide where to locate your beginning point—is it to be at the back, the center, the side (left or right), downstage somewhere, or will your dance begin offstage? Once the starting point has been decided upon, where is it going to lead? What path will your dance take? What kinds of imaginary designs will you weave as you change directions? One pattern merges into another—from a circle to a zigzag to a square to a triangle—this merging makes less exact patterns that tend to be more interesting because they are not as predictable. You need to know something about the relative merits of various points on stage so that you know when it is best to carry your design forward, when to move it to a remote corner, and when to bring it to the center. In the book *The Art of Making Dances*, Doris Humphrey perceptively analyzed the comparative importance of the various stage areas. Such knowledge will be useful to you as you plan your design.

As a simple rule of thumb, there are six weak areas and seven strong ones on a stage (see diagram). Also add the fact that movement, though personal on the footlights and therefore only suitable for intimate moods, loses power as it retreats upstage—except at dead center. Remember that the main paths which are illuminated, so to speak, are the diagonals and down the center; that the sides are very weak for either entrances or exits, or any movement.[1]

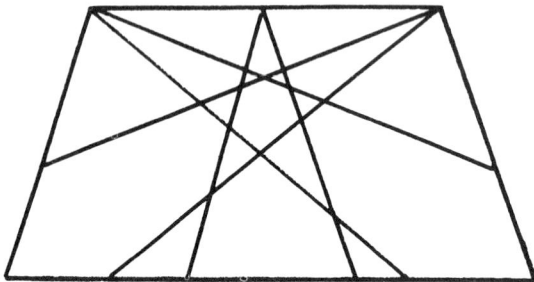

1. From *The Art Of Making Dances* by Doris Humphrey. Edited by Barbara Pollack. Line drawings by Stuyvesant Van Veen. Copyright © 1959 by Charles F. Woodford and Barbara Pollack. Reprinted and reproduced by permission of Holt, Rinehart & Winston, Inc.

Always impose your floor pattern on a real or imagined stage. Designs should be planned for theatrical presentation, for movement that is to be seen by an audience.

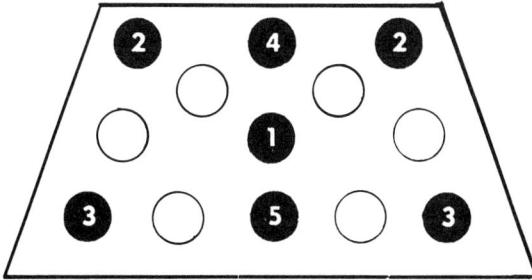

Relative Strengths of Stage Areas[2]

The *contained* design aspect has to do with volume and the way space takes on different shapes as it is confined and compressed. The silent stage, the empty dance space, has a volume that is contained within the actual exterior limits of walls, ceiling, and floor. It is three-dimensional, having length, breadth, and width. It is subject to change only as something takes place within it to remold it and to create new barriers. When placed within the stage volume, a single dancer or a single object such as a chair or a screen splits it into a new form. In working within the contained volume, we become aware of the shape of the distance between the dancer and the two sides of the stage and the relationship of the dancer or object to the back curtain, the footlights, the top of the proscenium, and the floor.

The spaces that are created between dancers also give volume shape, as does the contained space defined by the lines of the body instrument or the floor pattern. As in all design aspects of dance, these volume shapes constantly change. As the movements set up new relationships, the volume is transformed. Think of two dancers standing at opposite ends of a diagonal line. Between them is a rather large volume of space. As they move closer together the space between them is compressed. As they draw nearer, this action psychologically produces a sense of increased tension. Invisible lines seem to begin to connect the two and to become progressively more taut. The opposite effect also should be noted: the volume is expanded as two objects retreat from one another, and the sensations become those of diminishing tensions. Stage volumes change not only shape and dimension, but also intensity.

2. Ibid.

A knowledge of how to work with the third dimension is absolutely indispensable in the manipulation of volume. Patterns must be given depth. Straight side-to-side patterns might be acceptable in the domain of the chorus line, but even here the results often are rather dull and ordinary. Imagine the mundane effect of two dancers who always maintain the same distance between themselves and the front of the stage. What they do would appear flat and two-dimensional because it would lack depth. Now visualize what would happen as soon as one dancer moved toward the back of the stage and crossed behind the first dancer. The third dimension suddenly would come to life, and you would become aware of in-depth relationships. It does not take two or more dancers to add the third dimension to dance movement, for even a soloist does this as soon as he moves in any direction other than sideways, or even when he moves a part of his body in depth, such as when he makes an arm or leg gesture toward one of the stage corners. A simple and effective way of establishing the third dimension is to have one dancer in the group pass between two others. If you are striving to obtain the effect of flatness when you are working with a problem that deals with the primitive or one that refers to a Greek frieze, then you might decide to avoid the third dimension, but this would be done with purpose.

Let us now consider the *temporal* aspect of design as it relates to dance. As mentioned previously, the continuum of dance movement is of such nature that motifs must be evolving constantly. Each pattern is formulated and then dissolved, to be succeeded by a fresh one. Dance takes place within a span of time, and within that span there should be an orderly arrangement of its patterns. Beginning choreographers tend to crowd too many brief designs into too short a length of time. These need to be extended and prolonged, drawn out like a linen thread for the weaving. Then the final dance tapestry will be clear and uncluttered, and its patterns will be skillfully interwoven. The eye cannot follow movement patterns that shift too quickly; this is the reason legerdemain is successful—"The hand is quicker than the eye." There should be sufficient time allocated to the development of a design so that it can be absorbed visually.

Temporal design frequently is related to the timing of actual experience. Situations and emotional states have a time plan that must be taken into consideration. Imagine, for example, that you are waiting for an important phone call. The longer the wait, the more the tensions increase. However, if the suspense is prolonged beyond a certain point of time in a dance, interest will flag. Think of the timing of a situation in which you have misplaced your notebook and find that it is time to leave for class. Here you might want to use many small patterns in order to convey a sense of distraction. Awareness of the principle of psychological timing of actual experiences and reactions will help give a dramatic continuity to your dance. You may want to depart from a too-literal sense of timing (this is ordinarily the case), but do use it to supply some of the clues that will make your patterns effectively meaningful.

The fourth aspect, *structural* design, has to do with the shaping of the total form of a composition. Like music, a dance composition follows a specific plan of organization in fitting together its various sections. It must achieve a sense of unity and at the same time have sufficient variety in order to be interesting. Many dances use the same structure as their musical counterparts do. The simplest structural form is the AB, composed of two sections that are related but contrasting. Because of its balanced order, one of the most satisfying structures is the ABA¹. Here there still are two contrasting sections, but the dance is brought to a conclusion by a restatement of the original or first section. Your dance idea might lend itself to the structural pattern represented by ABACADAEAF, like a song of many verses with but a single refrain. Many other combinations are possible, such as ABCBA, ABBA, ABCAC, or the theme and variations form, represented as AA¹A²A³A⁴, in which each restatement of the original theme is given a fresh slant. It is only when you begin to assemble several longer movement phrases that you will be involved with total structure, but as you watch a finished dance composition, try to discover the structure that the choreographer had in mind.

What are the principles of a good design? How do we know what to select? What is considered aesthetically pleasing as opposed to that which is regarded as poor design? First, we should bear in mind that values change from one era to the next. Today we reveal the function by discarding the extraneous; at another time, we disguised it. Today we are interested in the handcrafted, the homespun, and the natural products of our environment, but tomorrow we might return to the artificial ornateness of the baroque or the sleek sophistication of the 1950s. While once we dreamed of owning a Thunderbird, today we would prefer to travel in a VW van. What is "in" today will be "out" tomorrow, for styles and tastes fluctuate. The artist is sensitive to the aesthetics of his time, adjusting his style to conform to time's changing face.

There are, however, some basic principles that underlie all good dance design. *Simplicity* is one of the most important. The competent choreographer uses his materials sparingly, with precise clarity. He does not overcrowd his designs by trying to use his entire vocabulary of movement. He selects a few movements that are appropriate to his idea, and then he manipulates them in many ways. A movement design that is initiated by one part of the body might then be taken up by another body segment. A circling arm pattern might at some point be carried by the leg, for example. The level of a pattern might be changed. It might be done from a kneeling position and then from a standing one. It might be performed axially, that is to say, in place, and then it might be carried through space as a locomotor pattern. The temporal duration of a design might be long and then short or slow and then fast. A floor pattern might move forward and then be reversed in the same way a film is rewound on its reel. A design might begin as a small thing and then gradually expand as, for instance, a small circular path that continually widens as it is repeated. The design can be interestingly varied by changing its rhythm, its force, or its dynamics. The manipulation of a relatively few movements is the real secret of successful dance design.

In designing interesting and meaningful movement, the choreographer deals with another important principle, that of balance. This coin has two faces, the *symmetrical* and the *asymmetrical*. The symmetrical side is reposeful, serene, and classic; the asymmetrical is disturbing, restless, and unstable. As human beings, when we want comfort and security we gravitate toward the symmetrical; its perfection of balance invokes the feeling of stability and makes us feel that we are standing on two feet, confidently and contentedly. Art, however, has another mission to perform. Its purpose is to excite, astonish, and even at times irritate in order to stimulate reaction. Its intention is to awaken responses, avoid the placid, and deal with unrest, not with repose. It does not want to lull its audience to sleep but, instead, to stir it into active response. Therefore, movements that are asymmetrical are planned for dance, particularly modern dance, because they convey a sense of excitement and unpredictability, of action and dramatic interplay. Yet beginning choreographers have a tendency to latch on to symmetricality like a security blanket. The world that man has made for himself may be predominantly symmetrical—his buildings, his furniture, his city planning, his motor cars—but nature is not unless man intercedes. What tree is symmetrically perfect, what shrub or plant, what outcropping of rock? Man's own body is not symmetrical even though he has two ears, two arms, and two legs. One eyebrow might be slightly higher than its companion, the mouth a bit crookedly one-sided, and even the natural part of the hair may be more to the left than to the right. Few people are entirely ambidextrous—we are right- or left-handed (and -footed). These "imperfections" lend an interest to the design—a certain unexpectedness.

Symmetry for dance should not be ruled out completely, but it is suggested that you develop a working habit of avoiding it in favor of the asymmetrical as much as possible. Symmetry does have a place. There will be moments in a dance when things should come to rest—when conflict is resolved and there is pause. It might well be used as a point of departure, at the start of an opening statement of grandeur, for instance. It can be authoritative, majestic, and imposing, but it should be used sparingly.

Another useful rule of thumb is related to group composition. In general, the greater the number of dancers, the simpler the movement design must be. The eye cannot take in too much at any given time. If five or six performers are each given separate and involved movement patterns, the effect is chaotic. This is not to say that they should move simply and in unison at all times, but neither should they go their separate ways. This becomes distracting and incoherent. There should be unity as well as variety and an overall contrived and telling simplicity in the composition. If a soloist is to be supported by a group, then it becomes essential that the group action be minimized unless, of course, the choreographic intent is to absorb or destroy the individual.

In this brief chapter it has not been possible to deal with the subject of design in depth. At best, in a few pages it is possible to offer only a few suggestions for your consideration. Train your eyes to see and to be sensitive to the designs with which our lives are surrounded. Examine the detail in nature—in the gnarled trunk of an old oak, in a fingerprint, in the formations of clouds, or the flames from a wood fire. As a dancer, you must train not only your instrument to move, but also your ears to hear and your eyes to see.

DO IT YOURSELF

Floor Patterns for a Solo Dancer

Draw a continuous line from one dot to the other using the stage area creatively. Make the design interesting.

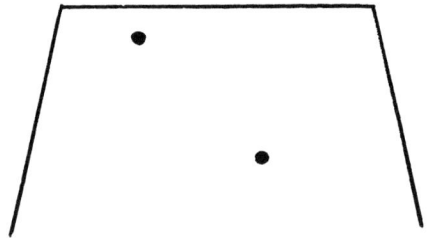

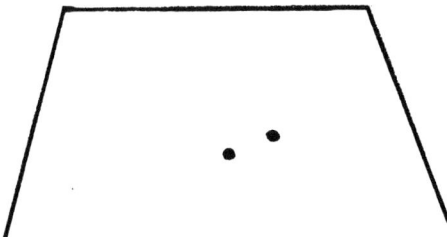

DO IT YOURSELF

Floor Patterns for Two Dancers

Draw continuous lines through the stage area from dot to dot and x to x. Use two different colors to keep each pattern distinct.

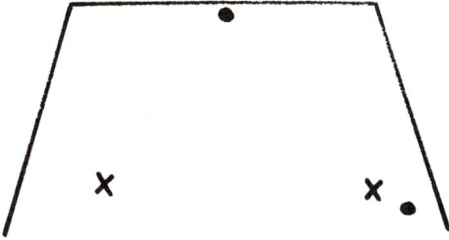

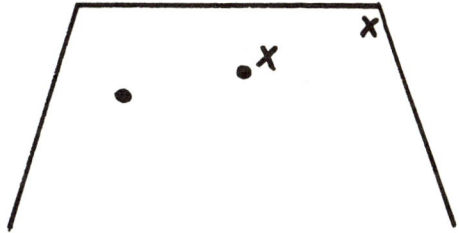

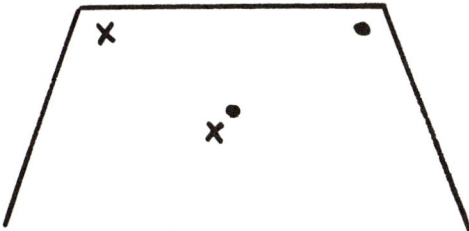

Notes on performing

11

Contemporary Music Notation

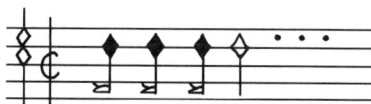

Sixteenth-Century Music Notation

As a beginning dancer, even if you are talented, you will not be ready to perform on stage until you have taken more classes, spent a great deal of time in preparation, and rehearsed, rehearsed, rehearsed. Nonetheless, you should be oriented to performance from the start; acquire the habit of being constantly aware of what you are doing and how it might look to an audience. Dance is a performing art. Even the beginner should adopt the attitude of a professional dancer and concentrate on every movement he makes. The exception is during times of improvisation. Performance demands not only concentration, but sensitivity, discrimination, selectivity, imagination, and above all, hard work. To perform for an audience is a privilege, not a right. You will have to earn this privilege, and this will take time.

From the very first moment of the dance experience, you are preparing for the ultimate goal—communicative performance. That privileged moment when the lights go on and the curtain rises will come. Long before it does, you will be performing for others. During some lesson, you will be called upon to show what you are doing to the other members of your class. This may be difficult for you to do at first, but you will never experience the thrill of an audience's warm applause until you are able to handle this moment of truth, to stand alone as others watch you dance. You might dread this experience to some degree; most people do. But if you analyze your feelings, you will recognize that they really stem from a fear of failure. If you allow yourself to become anxious when you are called upon to come before the class, you will be unable to perform at your best. Anxiety produces tension, and tension will distort and inhibit your movements. How can you meet this challenge? How do you help yourself do your best?

The problem is threefold: first, you must know what you are doing; second, you must stop thinking about yourself and concentrate on thinking about the movements; and third, you must instill confidence in your audience.

Knowing has to do with understanding. If you have listened carefully to the directions given by your dance instructor, and if you have been aware of your movement responses and subjected them to self-evaluation, you will have gained in understanding. Certainly you will have to practice movements again and again until you can perform them with ease. You will have to prance across the floor many times until it becomes efficient and leap a hundred leaps until your timing, your use of force, and your control over your entire body are such that you seem to soar without effort. Your mistakes should not discourage you—you should continue the attempt. If you are not satisfied with your progress, seek assistance from your instructor. He or she is best qualified to spot your difficulties and to suggest what you can do to correct them. Do not attempt to disguise your problems or to cover up inadequacies or run away from them. If you are in trouble, seek help. Move with understanding. If you knew all there is to know about dance, you would not be taking a class. Learning is progress and continuous acquisition of new pieces of information; teaching is assisting learners in developing insights and in handling the materials of dance effectively. You will not be called upon to perform until you have an adequate knowledge of that which is to be performed.

The redirection from thinking of self is never easy. We habitually think, How do I look? What does she think of me? What should I say? Self-doubts have a way of creeping into our consciousnesses. We must not extend guest privileges to them; we must not entertain or give them harbor. There is never room in the mind for more than one thought at any given instant. You do have the power to accentuate the positive and to eliminate the negative. Self-negation is self-destruction; self-affirmation is being at one's best, without conceit, but with sincerity of purpose.

Why is it so important for others to be confident of your performance? From what has been learned about the nature of human responses, we know that the spectator identifies with the performer, a process called *empathy*. People weep at the enactment of tragedy; they laugh at comedy. They become involved personally when they observe human suffering or human conflict, even when the situation is a make-believe one. Surely you have been agonized when one of your classmates has recited poorly. You must have shared his humiliation and his sense of defeat in some way. On the other hand, how good you must have felt when he did well! This is why you must be able to instill in others a confidence in your ability to perform the assigned task in the right way.

These are some of the suggestions that students have found helpful in attaining the confidence necessary to perform at their best. First, rest assured that you will not be invited to perform until you are ready to do so. When the moment arises, move easily into your starting position, crossing the floor with head and eyes high and your thoughts on the subject of the movement problem, not on yourself. When you reach the point at which you must begin (try to put the enchantment of distance between you and your audience), take a moment or two to get your audience's attention and to assemble your body and thoughts. Then make your opening gesture and from this moment on, *concentrate*; depend on concentration and muscle memory to see you through to the end. If the unforeseen happens, if you get off to a bad start and it is evident that you can not get back on the right track, stop and begin again. Whatever you do, do not apologize or offer excuses. As you perform, attend to your relationship with the accompaniment; it is your support, your connection with time. Do not be distracted by anything external to your dance movements— a cough or a laugh, the flapping of a window shade, or the rumbling of the radiator pipes. Stay within your movement at every single instant until it is complete; then pause (Do not bolt like a frightened deer!), count to three (to yourself, naturally), and with dignity walk out of the dancing space. Even after you have returned to your friends, to the anonymity of the group, do not collapse or give vent to any form of hysterical outburst. Your pulse rate will return to normal, your breathing will slow down, and your tensions will be released in short order. You have another assignment now as part of the audience for the next person who is to perform.

Do not resort to clowning, to playing the fool, in order to cover up your inadequacies. You are expected to give your best and to be at your best at all times.

We reveal so much of what we are by the way in which we move. Our physical instrument often takes on the shape of our thinking and feelings. You already have discovered this. Optimism is mirrored in the body, but so is defeat. Did you know that your thoughts and feelings can become a reflection of your body attitudes and the way you move? Try moving around in space with your head hanging, your arms limp, and your feet shuffling. How does this make you feel? Now do the opposite—move with your head up, arms swinging, and a lift to your walk, and notice the change inside you. This is a principle you should deal with as you are about to perform.

You are tested in modern dance by your performance; it is your challenge and your privilege. At some time you will be required to present something born of your invention and practice. Be ready for your moment of truth. Keep the following in mind:

1. *Be prepared.* Give sufficient thought and practice time to that which you are to perform. If necessary, put in extra time outside of class, at least in thinking through the problem.
2. *Contribute your best effort.* Set your performance standards high.
3. *Seek criticism and advice.* Accept the comments of those competent to judge and assist you.
4. *Employ self-appraisal.* Look at what you are doing as though you yourself were a spectator. Be discriminating and thoughtful.
5. *Concentrate.* Think only about what is being performed.
6. *Inspire confidence in others.* First instill it in yourself and then reflect it; others will then be certain of your strengths.
7. *Be gracious.* Accept commendations with grace and criticism with objectivity.

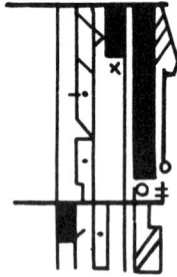

Labanotation

Looking at dance

12

Today there is greater opportunity than ever before to see modern dance performances. Not only can you find dance concert series being sponsored even by small communities throughout the country, but there also are many local adult and student groups offering concerts that are open to the public. Attending them will enrich your own dance experiences, providing you with ideas you can incorporate into your own experimentation and training you to look at dance discerningly.

Some critics claim that today's modern dance has lost stature and become devitalized and incoherent now that most of its pioneers have died. They hold the opinion that present-day choreographers have strayed too far from the mainstream of the art and that the period of greatness has ended. Others, however, maintain that we again are going through a period of searching, and that this is inevitable as modern dance adjusts to its present time. More than half a century has gone by since modern dance became established as a new art form, and it may be that we, in this time of transition, are nearing the threshold of new greatness. As you look at the new choreographies, bear in mind the unalterable fact that dance cannot change its basic purpose. *Art is communication.*

In the beginning, young modern dance choreographers had to struggle against a tendency to be too literal and to avoid the pitfalls of storytelling and pantomimic gestures. They had to invent new movements that approached the abstract. But now that we have an extensive movement vocabulary, perhaps we should question the abstractions. Are meanings being obscured in these attempts to dehumanize human movements? Even when a performer is encased in a strangely shaped structure such as the ones Alwyn Nicolais places upon his dancers, audiences must remain aware that within the form there is a living, breathing human being.

Perhaps we also have placed too great an emphasis on individuality and not enough on responsibility. When a dance is too personal, too involved with the psyche of the choreographer that it becomes a means of therapy, where does an audience come in? Who cares? A dance might be motivated by personal suffering or sorrow, but then the choreographer has the responsibility of transforming the work into the realm of universal suffering or sorrow so that an audience can appreciate and relate to it, too.

At the absolute top of the list of irresponsible creations are works that are misrepresented as dance in order to lure an audience into the theatre. Can you be entertained by a dancer standing in the middle of the stage who slowly bites into an apple, taking ten minutes to do so, and then throws the core over the footlights? Or by a seemingly endless number during which your ears are blasted by electronic sound raised beyond the level of human comfort as you watch three people wind and unwind balls of colored yarn? There are a few performing groups whose sole purpose, apparently, is audience put-down, who operate from a premise of contempt and disregard and at the same time consider themselves avant-garde.

There are works, frankly experimental, that depart from the usual format and at the same time provide audience interest and stimulation, such as those labeled *multimedia*. Although these presentations are at the opposite pole from the pure dance, it may be that a new art form is evolving as the various elements of sound, slide projections, film clips, beams of light, gadgets, and human bodies are blended together. Sometimes so much is going on at one time that the viewer becomes confused and distracted, but when there is an established relationship between the various elements, the results can be effective.

The traditionally dance-like dance is a pleasant way of providing relief in a program of heavier works. The audience does not have to be involved with meanings and content and can relax and enjoy the unfolding of movement patterns and designs. Successful dances belonging to this category sustain a visual interest throughout by a skillful application of the principles of good design and beautiful movements. The dance-like dance demands nothing from its audience except receptivity of its visual manifestations.

As you continue your study of modern dance, you will discover that you not only are training your body to move, but you also are teaching your eyes to see. You will begin to look at dance with discernment and to formulate value judgments about it that are based upon the knowledge you have acquired. You probably have begun to realize already that the human body is capable of producing an infinite number of designs within time and space, and that the choreographer is faced with the task of selecting those movements that are both visually interesting and appropriate for the communication of his or her idea. Your own creative efforts will become more interesting as you explore the qualities of movement and learn to employ dynamic changes to provide greater subtlety to your compositions. Each meeting of the class gives you the opportunity to develop your critical ability to look at dance, for as you establish criteria for your own work, you are developing a sense of values.

Too often we think of criticism as something essentially negative or destructive. Actually, criticism is for the purpose of revealing the truth. The thing being criticized might need to be torn apart before it can become good. It is essential that we negate that which is false, affected, insincere, and meaningless if we are to have standards of excellence. The discarded dance materials of our greatest choreographers would fill warehouses. The process is one of trial and error that sometimes seems endless. But eventually we can bring forth something of worth. Subject your own efforts to self-criticism first, and then when there is an opportunity to perform for others, be willing to accept their suggestions. Sometimes even though a movement feels right, it is not. Even though you understand its meaning, it does not communicate to those who are watching. Evaluation by your instructor and your classmates can be helpful in suggesting ways you can become more articulate with movement. Pearls are not contained in every oyster; throw away the empty shells and keep on searching.

During the process of constructing your own patterns of dance movement, establish some criteria that will enable you to look at your own efforts with objectivity. You might ask yourself questions such as the following:

1. Are my movement designs interesting and appropriate?
2. Have I avoided natural gestures without losing the communication of my idea? Am I avoiding familiar techniques or at least using them in a fresh way?
3. Are my rhythms interesting, or are they pedestrian and overly repetitious?
4. Have I used too much material, or have I achieved the effect of the economy of means?
5. Did I solve the problem to the best of my ability?

6. Have I revealed the extent of my technical range? Have I demanded too little or too much? Can I perform these movements efficiently but with a certain amount of daring?

7. Have I observed principles of contrast and variety without straying from the subject?

8. Have I established an interesting relationship between the movements and the accompaniment and avoided responding to it on a note-for-note basis? Have I supplied a counterpoint of movement?

9. Does the study have a sense of unity and wholeness? Have I made transitions smoothly so that all parts seem to develop logically?

Your study of modern dance should equip you to become a discerning member of the dance audience, for you will acquire a deeper understanding of what is essential for dance to become communicative. There might not be many opportunities in your community to see a live concert, but dance is an important ingredient of many movies and television shows. Each time you watch it, apply what you have learned to the viewing. Develop your ability to discriminate between what is artistic and what is mediocre. At the professional level, mediocrity is not acceptable, although we do look with tolerance upon the works of the amateur and continue to support student endeavors. At the professional level, dance should come closer to the ideal, even though a true masterpiece will be rare. A good dance—a well-constructed composition, flawlessly performed—is to be expected from professionals. Compare your reactions with those of the reviewers. Read what the critics have to say, but only after you have formed your own opinions. You might or might not agree. The important thing is that you observe dance with a deep insight and go beyond thinking, I liked or I did not like that number. Use the knowledge you have acquired about dance as you search for explanations and reasons why one composition is appealing and another is not.

Examine the elements that contribute to the support of the dance—the costuming, the lighting, and the scenery. Do they contribute to the whole? Are they used in a subtle way? Sometimes these elements overpower or encumber the dance, even distract from it by competing for your attention. Scenery, accompaniment, costumes, and lighting must maintain the position of backing up the dance. They are the servants whose ministrations are helpful but whose roles must be subordinate. They function with discretion and focus their talents on enhancing the dance. There should be a unity of the entire production, a harmonious wholeness of the technical and the creative.

When there is an opportunity for you to attend a full-length modern dance concert, take advantage of it. Test your critical ability. Select from the program those numbers you considered outstanding. Why did they interest you? Would you like to see them repeated? How were the various dances programmed? Program planners sometimes have difficulty, particularly with dances that are good openers. Was there a rhythm to the plan and sufficient contrast and variety to the numbers? Were the dances too long to sustain your interest? Were titles and program notes helpful? Which performers stood out? Why? Was the pacing of the concert good, or were there long waits between numbers? What improvements could be made, and what would you suggest to the choreographers?

If you enjoyed the performance, let the artists know you did. Everyone likes approval. After the final curtain falls, drop in backstage to offer your congratulations. This is especially meaningful if some of your friends are in the cast; they will appreciate your thoughtfulness. The professional dance artist also is pleased to receive your approval in this immediate way.

As an intelligent member of a dance audience, view each performance with understanding. Increase your own satisfaction by training yourself to be actively discerning. Even though your place is a seat in the balcony, you in a sense also are performing. Recognize what is good in dance and give it your support. Introduce some of your friends to a dance experience. The audience for dance is important to its continued existence as a performing art. You are important to this existence, for you can provide encouragement and performing opportunities for the dance artists of the future.

Two on the aisle

13

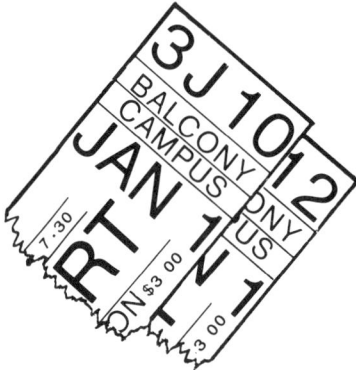

As a result of your initial high school or college dance experience, you are eligible to join those dedicated dance buffs who form the main body of the dance audiences that have sprung up everywhere. You are better prepared to receive the messages of the professional dance artists with understanding. The next time a professional dance company visits your community, buy tickets for yourself and a friend. Complete your dance study by viewing the finished product.

Much of the fascination of any theatrical presentation is its aura of mystery. A dance performance is particularly provocative because it consciously is removed from the real and the everyday, yet by implication it deals with the familiar. The trained dancer appears to be a superbeing whose body is capable of moving in incredible ways. His leaps defy the laws of gravity, and he has a sense of timing with the mechanical accuracy of a finely precisioned watch. Movements that you know demand the utmost exertion are performed with ease and aplomb. Your eyes drink in visual patterns of inestimable beauty that are continually evolving and dissolving as the focal point of the dance shifts from one point of emphasis to another. A part of your brain insists that you are viewing the impossible, but another part tells you that every dancer and choreographer started at the beginning, just as you did.

Because of your own experience, you are able to better understand the rituals being enacted on the stage. You have trained your eyes to observe the details that combine to form the whole. You have been through many of the processes that dancers and choreographers must undergo in the preparation of a completed composition. You also know how essential it is for every dancer to be technically proficient without sacrificing the individual uniqueness he or she imparts to the role. You have constructed small fragments of composition, so you can appreciate what goes into a major work that plays for a mere twenty or thirty minutes.

By the time a choreographer has translated an idea into reality, the dancers have rehearsed, the costumes, accompaniment, lighting, and details of staging have been worked out, a theater has been rented, publicity has gone out, and tickets have been sold, months have gone into the preparation of a concert—months and energy and dedication. The harmony of the total production depends upon the special talents of many people working together with a sense of mutual respect and total involvement in the success of the outcome. The choreographer is responsible for the artistic unity of the production and depends not only on the members of the company, but also on the production staff for the presentation. Dance is a jewel. Its setting must be carefully wrought if it is to reveal its greatest beauty and deepest meaning. Your applause should acknowledge not only what you have seen, but also what you know has gone into the making.

Dance is the most ephemeral of the arts as well as the most impermanent. It happens only once in a particular way. If you were to attend the same concert night after night, your responses would differ every time, and each dance on the program also would have altered its appearance to some extent. There is no absolute constancy in human behavior; audiences and dancers react and respond differently with each passing moment in time. The performer strives for those moments of rapport with an audience when there is easy communication. They happen, but only when the gods are smiling.

Today's audiences have the opportunity of seeing some of the great dance compositions of the past, like Martha Graham's *Primitive Mysteries* (1931), Agnes de Mille's *Rodeo*, and Doris Humphrey's *Passacaglia*. Many of the professional dance companies and even college dance groups are going through a period of revival, recreating the monumental works that were choreographed by the pioneer artists of the thirties and forties. In these restorations, you have a chance to see compositions that have withstood the passage of time—the classic masterpieces of the modern dance world. They cannot be exact replicas of the originals, but in many instances they are better performed. Today, the average company member is better trained technically than one of past decades. However, the solo performers for the most part are unable to impart a sense of supreme artistry to the roles first danced by José Limón, Martha Graham, and Doris Humphrey. The unquestionable explanation is because these roles were choreographed by the artists for themselves; they were inextricably connected to their own unique beings, based upon the capabilities of their individual instruments and inner spirits. What you will see now is a translation—hopefully a good one.

The total amount of box office receipts for a dance performance pays for only a small fraction of the cost of the performance. This is the reason so few modern dance companies have been able to stay together, let alone go on tour. The bread-and-butter aspects force dance artists to fend for themselves unless their company has the backing of an "angel" or is subsidized by a governmental grant or agency. It is a startling fact that no permanent group of dance artists can sustain its unity through performances without outside financial aid. The soloist you see tonight may have been working at Macy's during the day or have spent the afternoon teaching children's classes at the Y or auditioning for a nightclub act. Unless the dancer is a member of Equity, he seldom is paid for rehearsals. Fortunately, the situation today is being remedied somewhat. There is more subsidy and more genuine concern about the preservation and encouragement of those arts that contribute to our national culture. Many people who deserve this support have not yet received it, however.

If you wish to attend professional modern dance performances frequently, you will need to go to New York. Except for an infrequent tour of one-night stands, such as the special event series sponsored by your university, professional concerts are limited to the Broadway or off-Broadway locales. Even there, the season is short. Martha Graham's company played for three weeks in the fall of 1965. This was the longest run in its thirty-five year history! Younger artists may bring dance to your community, for the hardships of a tour will be offset for them by their eagerness to build a following. Typical of the one-night-stand tour is the following experience:

At the invitation of the concert committee of a Midwestern university, two relatively unknown but talented modern dance artists were invited to present a concert on campus. The university theater was undergoing extensive alterations, so it was necessary to use the gymnasium for the performance, seating the audience on temporary bleachers and converting the basketball court into a stage. The dancers arrived at midnight by train from New York, having waited several hours at midpoint to transfer to the line that took them to their final destination. The local station was closed, so the welcoming committee pitched in to get their trunks and suitcases out of the baggage car and into station wagons. Everything was transported to the gymnasium, where costumes were unpacked and hung up, props were checked, and plans for rehearsal and performance were gone over. Then the dancers were driven to the student union to catch a few hours of much needed sleep. Early the next morning they were hard at work, helping a student crew prepare the improvised stage, devising places for exits and entrances with screens, defining the stage area with tape, locating striplights and a few spotlights and floodlights for illumination, and preparing cue sheets for the running of the show. The dancers then had a run-through to adjust to the space and to rehearse the sound and light cues. After a hurried lunch, costumes were pressed and hung up in the order of the performance, a few necessary repairs were made on the props, the sound levels were checked, and the cue sheets were revised; then students began arriving for a master class. After teaching an exciting hour-and-one-half lesson, the young artists dashed back to the student union, changed clothes, and appeared as guests of honor at a faculty reception. Back in the converted office that served as a dressing room, they had a sandwich-and-soup dinner before putting on their makeup and getting into costume for the first dance number. After thirty minutes of warming-up techniques, it was show time. Harried, hurried, and exhausting? Of course, but the wonder of it all is that from the moment the two appeared on the improvised stage until they disappeared into the wings, there was no hint of what had gone into the preparation. The concert was controlled, effortless, and artistically satisfying. Furthermore, their ordeal did not end with the applause, for immediately afterward the costumes and props were gathered up and packed back into their trunks, the dancers showered hurriedly, removed their make-up, and put on their traveling shoes, for they had to catch that same midnight train which carried them to the place where they would be performing the next night.

Although you will be able to see good modern dance in films and on television, there is no substitute for the live experience, so buy a ticket whenever the opportunity presents itself, or volunteer to usher if your funds are running low. Enjoy the spectacle of the performance even though you are aware of the real hardships that have preceded the finished product. Realize that a dancer has chosen this way of life because of a compelling need to communicate the uniqueness of his being through dance. The agony of the preparation is forgotten the moment the curtain rises and the dancer prepares to step on stage. The act of communication is complete when he becomes acutely aware that, in the words of Martha Graham, ". . . there is only one of you in all of time."[1]

1. Martha Graham, in souvenir concert program, 1965.

Pilgrim's progress

14

As you take this first journey in modern dance, as you train your body instrument to carry you upon the excursion and your mind to interpret the signs, you will obtain at least a glimpse of the dancer's world. New vistas will be opened up to you as you complete your first dance course. You might begin asking yourself, Where shall I go next? You might discover that you would like to take another trip and be guided along avenues that will lead you further. Introductory courses open only the first pathways but well might whet your appetite for more advanced work. Most high schools, colleges, and universities offer courses that go beyond the beginning level in modern dance: intermediate and advanced technique, composition, rhythmic analysis, and music for dance, for example. You might now be interested in the technical or design aspect of dance and want to learn how to light a dance concert or how to design costumes and apply makeup. Many institutions offer courses in notation, which is a method for recording movements and complete choreographies. Some beginning students discover they have become interested in dance as a teaching profession and enter the professional curriculum that is designed to prepare them for this field.

Even though you may decide not to take another credit course in dance, you might enjoy extracurricular dance experiences such as becoming a member of the modern dance club on your campus or reading some of the interesting books that have been written about dance and dancers. Your instructor can add to those listed in the Appendix. Some communities have excellent programs in modern dance that include recreational classes, performing groups, or dance film series. You might like to spend a summer studying dance in a concentrated way and receiving instruction from professional dance artists. There are many places throughout the country where

this is possible. Again, your instructor can advise you and also explain how to apply for scholarships. After you have completed your first course, you have not reached the end of the road.

As you study the art that is modern dance, there are things you can do yourself to hasten your progress and add to your understanding and appreciation of dance. Visit other classes; drop in at a dance rehearsal; sit in on a master class or, better yet, take part in one when it is offered; go to a modern dance concert, even one given by nonprofessionals; discuss dance with some professional students; and whenever possible, practice your techniques.

To help you profit fully from your experience in class, here are a few suggestions:

1. Be prepared and alert from the moment you enter the dance studio so that you are open to receiving instruction.
2. Respond with spontaneity.
3. Be sure you understand all directions.
4. Concentrate on the moves you are performing. Maintain mental control over your instrument, your body.
5. Give this instrument the best of care. Practice good health habits, give it proper nourishment and rest, and protect it from abuse.
6. Contribute to the success of the class. Work not only for yourself, but be helpful to others.
7. Be meticulous about your movements; set standards for yourself that are high but attainable.
8. Expect enjoyment from the experience of learning to move well and meaningfully.

In ten years, if you have practiced and studied dance for four or five hours a day, you might become a professional artist; but after even one beginning course in modern dance, you will be prepared to share in its communion as a member of an audience and to be a part of the art experience.

A basic vocabulary

Parsley, persevering in a tree,
Maturely withers in the alchemy
Of elms and willows. So with us,
The elementary is most serious.

Around the Fish: After Paul Klee
by Howard Moss

Axial-locomotor. Refers to performance of in-place techniques (axial) and techniques used to change location (locomotor). In the first instance, the body moves on its own vertical axis; in the second, movement is across the floor.

Basic axial movements. Simple motions of the body common to all physical activities. These include bending, twisting, rotating, and swaying.

Basic locomotor movements. Simple step patterns common to all forms of dance. These include sliding, skipping, running, hopping, and jumping.

Bounces. Action similar to a bouncing ball. The impulse of the movement is downward and is followed by a rebound. Often used during warm-up period.

Brushes. A technique for strengthening ankles and legs. Action involves lifting and returning the straight leg, keeping the foot in contact with the floor as long as possible.

Contraction-release. A movement principle basic to Graham's technique involving the shortening (contraction) and lengthening (release) of muscles.

Dance walk. Reverse from normal "heel first" walk. Ball of foot strikes the floor at the beginning of the step and is followed by the heel; turn-out is emphasized as well as smoothness.

var *Limón walk.* A style of dance walk associated with the Limón technique. The back foot maintains contact with floor, while passing through to the forward position. Rib cage is held high.

Fall-recovery. Controlled response to pull of gravity downward (fall) and a return response against gravity (recovery). An important element of the Humphrey-Weidman technique, and one which can be performed in any direction or as a spiral.

First, second, third, fourth, and fifth positions. Adopted from the classical ballet, these refer to positions of feet and arms. Used to vary techniques and extend the range of a movement.

Flex-extend. Similar to contraction-release or bend-and-stretch. Muscles are shortened (flexed) and lengthened (extended).

Half-toe. A partial *relevé* with the heel raised off the floor and the body weight supported by the ball of the foot.

Leap. A propulsive movement into the air with a transfer of weight from the take-off foot to the landing foot. The emphasis can be vertical or horizontal. Ankles and knees can be flexed or extended while body is in the air.

Plié-relevé. From the French "to bend" and "to lift," this is one of the most important of all dance techniques. Action is centered at the hip, knee, and ankle joints, and emphasis is on good alignment of spine and pelvis. Body is lowered (*plié*) and lifted (*relevé*) by flexion and extension of the feet and legs in a vertical line.

Prance. A locomotor technique; variant of running. Free leg is lifted forward, knee flexed, ankle extended. The movement is sharp and precise.

Push-off. Pressure against an object such as the floor that adds extra impulse to a movement.

Rib cage. That part of the body protected and surrounded by the ribs, sternum (breastbone), and scapulae (shoulder blades).

Triplet. A step combination similar to a waltz except that each of the three steps is taken in an open position. Accent is usually on the first of each three steps with a slight *plié*.

Turn-out. Rotation of legs outward from the hip joint; increases movement potential of the legs.

A suggested reading list

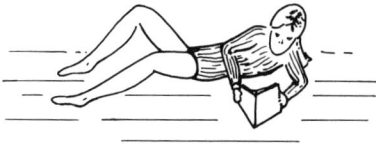

To supplement your study of modern dance, you might like to become acquainted with some of the dance literature, such as the books listed here. By no means is the list complete, but it is sufficient to provide you with a greater depth of understanding. Some of the books will be useful as you are taking the course in beginning modern dance; others will guide you along new pathways. Even though some books are now out of print, most libraries should have many of the following sources available.

General

COHEN, SELMA JEAN, ed. The Modern Dance, Seven Statements of Belief. Middletown, Conn.: Wesleyan University Press, 1966.

DE MILLE, AGNES. The Book of the Dance. New York: Golden Press, 1963.

———. To a Young Dancer. Boston: Little, Brown and Co., 1960.

HASKELL, ARNOLD. The Wonderful World of Dance. Garden City, New York: Garden City Books, 1960.

LLOYD, MARGARET. The Borzoi Book of Modern Dance. New York: Alfred A. Knopf, 1949.

MARTIN, JOHN. John Martin's Book of the Dance. New York: Tudor Publishing Co., 1963.

———. The Dance. New York: Tudor Publishing Co., 1946.

ROCHLEIN, HARVEY. Notes on Contemporary American Dance. Baltimore: University Extension Press, 1964.

SORRELL, WALTER. The Dance Has Many Faces. Cleveland: World Publishing Co., 1951.

———. The Dance Through the Ages. New York: Grosset and Dunlap, 1967.

TERRY, WALTER. *The Dance in America.* New York: Harper and Brothers, 1956, (rev. 1971).
WIGMAN, MARY. *The Language of Dance.* Middletown, Conn.: Wesleyan University Press, 1966.

Techniques and Composition

CHENEY, GAY, and STRADER, JANET. *Modern Dance.* Boston: Allyn and Bacon, Inc., 1969.
ELLFELDT, LOIS. *A Primer for Choreographers.* Palo Alto, Calif.: National Press Books, 1967.
———, and CARNES, EDWIN. *Dance Production Handbook.* Palo Alto, Calif.: National Press Books, 1967.
HAWKINS, ALMA M. *Creating through Dance.* Englewood Cliffs, N. J.: Prentice-Hall, Inc., 1964.
HAYES, ELIZABETH R. *Dance Composition and Production for High Schools and Colleges.* New York: Ronald Press Co., 1954.
HORST, LOUIS. *Pre-Classic Dance Forms.* New York: Kamin Dance Publishers, 1954.
———, and RUSSELL, CAROL. *Modern Dance Forms in Relation to the Other Modern Arts.* San Francisco: Impulse Publications, 1961.
HUMPHREY, DORIS. *The Art of Making Dances.* Edited by Barbara Pollack. New York: Holt, Rinehart, and Winston, Inc., 1959.
LIPPINCOTT, GERTRUDE, ed. *Dance Production.* Washington, D.C.: The American Association for Health, Physical Education and Recreation, 1956.
LOCKHART, AILEEN, and PEASE, ESTHER E. *Modern Dance: Building and Teaching Lessons.* 4th ed. Dubuque, Iowa: Wm. C. Brown Co. Publishers, 1973.
MELCER, FANNIE HELEN. *Staging the Dance.* Dubuque, Iowa: Wm. C. Brown Co. Publishers, 1955.
PEASE, ESTHER E. *Louis Horst: His Theories on Modern Dance Composition.* Unpublished doctoral dissertation, available on loan from The University of Michigan Library, 1953.
RADIR, RUTH ANDERSON. *Modern Dance for the Youth of America.* New York: A. S. Barnes and Co., 1944.
SHURR, GERTRUDE, and YOCUM, RACHEL DUNAVEN. *Modern Dance Techniques and Teaching.* New York: A. S. Barnes and Co., 1949.
TURNER, MARGERY J. *Modern Dance for High School and College.* Englewood Cliffs, N. J.: Prentice-Hall Inc., 1957.

Biographical

ARMITAGE, MERLE. *Martha Graham.* Limited edition of 1,000 copies, privately printed, Los Angeles, 1937.
BACH, RUDOLF. *Das Mary Wigman-Werk.* Dresden: Carl Reissner, 1933. Untranslated from German.
COHEN, SELMA JEAN, ed. *Doris Humphrey, an Artist First.* Middletown, Conn.: Wesleyan University Press, 1972.
DE MILLE, AGNES. *Dance to the Piper.* Boston: Little, Brown and Co., 1952.
DUNCAN, ISADORA. *My Life.* New York: Boni and Liveright, 1927.
McDONAGH, DON. *Martha Graham: A Biography.* New York: Praeger, 1973.
MORGAN, BARBARA. *Martha Graham: Sixteen Dances in Photographs.* New York: Duell, Sloan, and Pearce, 1941.

St. Denis, Ruth. *An Unfinished Life*. London: George G. Harrap and Co., Ltd.

Steegmuller, Francis, ed. *Your Isadora: The Love Story of Isadora Duncan and Gordon Craig*. New York: Random House, 1974.

What do you think?

The following questions are designed to stimulate the user of this text to apply the contained information to his or her own experience and thinking. In this way, what is learned is related to self-awareness and becomes magnified and enhanced. The order of the questions closely follows the sequence of chapters.

1. What are some examples of movements you customarily use to communicate with others?
2. What rites of passage do we celebrate today? What rites of intensification?
3. What are some of the ways your body reacts spontaneously?
4. What customs do you follow that are rooted in your own cultural heritage?
5. Think of a specific instance in which you reversed your opinion about something. What caused you to do so?
6. Should there be a difference in the ultimate goals of the educator and the professional artist?
7. How are the changing needs of contemporary society being met in your community or on your campus?
8. Why do we cling to the past?
9. Are any two things in nature as alike as "two peas in a pod"? Look closely at any two similar parts of your body—your eyes, hands, or arms, for example.
10. Visualize someone you think moves well. What factors contribute to the overall pattern of movement?
11. What things about your physical instrument cannot be altered? What things can you change?
12. How does being physically fit contribute to an improved life-style?
13. If you were the parent of a small son, would you rather have him participate in sports than in dance? Why?
14. Do you consider any of the arts suitable professions for men? Which ones?
15. How much are you affected by the opinions of your peer group?

16. How do you feel about a person you consider a nonconformist?
17. Under what set of circumstances do you feel most confident?
18. How do you react to criticism?
19. Can you be critical of others without inducing their resentment?
20. How is your rate of learning accelerated?
21. When gravity no longer is a factor, as with activities in outer space, how is movement affected?
22. Does your energy level fluctuate during the day? Does this fluctuation follow a pattern, such as high in the mornings and low in the afternoons? Do you know why this happens, if it does?
23. How many parts of your body can you rotate?
24. What characteristics help you identify a friend from a distance?
25. Why should you practice movement techniques daily?
26. What happens to muscles that remain inactive over a long period of time?
27. What movement combinations (in dance) do you do better now as a result of practice?
28. Why should art go beyond achievement of technical virtuosity?
29. How frequently do you exercise your imagination?
30. Imagine yourself doing an utterly ridiculous, impossible thing.
31. What would happen if the world really were flat?
32. Watch a cloud formation and describe the things you can see in it.
33. What part does curiosity play in the world of discovery? Can you think of specific instances in which your curiosity has operated?
34. What have you discovered through curiosity?
35. Can you think of an accidental happening that led to an important discovery?
36. Whom do you consider the most creative person you know? Why?
37. What part does form play in the identification of objects?
38. Do you like things to be orderly and balanced? Why, or why not?
39. What are your reactions when something is about to fall?
40. What are the directional lines of balance? of imbalance?
41. Observe the space between two objects. Can you draw its design?
42. List the things you did successfully in your last dance class. Also make a list of the things you did not do well. Are you stimulated to work harder because of your successes or your failures?
43. Have you changed your way of looking at movement? How?
44. Try writing a critique of a dance concert or even a single dance composition.
45. What has your dance experience contributed to you as an individual?

Appendix: Questions and answers

A Note to Reader

Unlike most other physical activities, modern dance seeks to encourage individual reactions and responses rather than group conformity. Even the discipline of its techniques takes into account the unique differences of individual body structures. As a dancer, you must be encouraged to think, to explore, and to discover your own solutions to dance problems without too great a concern about "right" answers.

You should, however, be able to evaluate what you have learned from reading this book by attempting to answer the following questions or looking up the answers indicated by page reference.

COMPLETION-

1. *(Martha Graham)* is credited with starting the modern dance movement in the United States. (p. 6)
2. The Big Four of American modern dance are *(Martha Graham, Doris Humphrey, Hanya Holm and Charles Weidman)*.
3. *(Design or form)* results from the shaping of the elements of dance. (p. 7)
4. The dynamics of dance are affected by the *(application of force)* to the movements. (p. 26)
5. *(Placement)* is the term used to describe the conscious alignment of the various body segments. (p. 35)
6. The *(force)* principle influences the quality of movement. (p. 26)
7. Dance movement also is flavored by what Delsarte termed the *(law of the personality)*. (p. 31)
8. Techniques are for the purpose of *(developing skills and building a vocabulary of dance movements)*. (p. 32)
9. Dance can fulfill our basic need to *(communicate and express our thoughts and feelings)*. (p. 2)
10. *(Breath control)* lends support to dance movement. (p. 36)
11. The four types of body joints are the *(hinge, pivot, ball-and-socket, and ovoid)*. (p. 30)
12. A technique can be altered by changing its *(rhythm, direction, speed, or spatial design)*. (p. 33)

13. Images are constructed from the (memory of an experience). (p. 39)
14. Concepts and ideas are brought into focus by the development of a (design). (p. 50)
15. The designs created by the dancer's feet as he or she moves through space are referred to as (floor patterns). (p. 51)
16. The competent choreographer uses dance materials sparingly, selecting but a few movements and then (manipulating them). (p. 55)
17. (Volume) is transformed as new spatial relationships are developed. (p. 53)
18. The (choreographer) is responsible for the coordination of all elements pertaining to performance. (p. 71)
19. The implicit goal of dance is to (reflect its time). (p. 4)
20. A personal experience needs to be dealt with in terms of its (universality of meaning) if it is to be used for composition. (p. 66)

MATCHING

1. Doris Humphrey	3.	Eurhythmy
2. Martha Graham	5.	First modern dancer
3. Dalcroze	8.	Body talk
4. Laban	1.	Fall and recovery
5. Mary Wigman	6.	Legacy of dance freedom
6. Isadora Duncan	2.	Contraction and release
7. Suzanne Langer	4.	Notation
8. Sylvia Ashton-Warner	7.	Significant form

DISCUSSION STATEMENTS

1. Modern dance reflects the attitudes of the twentieth century toward art.
2. Communication in dance can be likened to "body-talk."
3. Competition against other than self is deemphasized in a dance class.
4. Individuality of solutions to posed problems is expected and encouraged.
5. Movement experimentation can begin with the first lesson.
6. Technical skill is a preparation for performance.
7. An informed audience completes the channel of communication for dance.
8. Creative unfoldment is sporadic and akin to nature.
9. Dance is a three-dimensional art form.
10. Asymmetry of design connotes action; symmetry evokes a sense of repose and quiescence.
11. Irregular rhythms are of greater interest than regular ones.
12. The masculine element in dance is equally as important as the feminine.
13. Design gives rise to the form.
14. Dance is of primary importance; its accompaniment is secondary.
15. Simplicity of movement is essential in designing for a large group.
16. Daydreaming is an essential part of the creative process.
17. Evidence supports the fact that the creative person conceptualizes readily.
18. Communication is the ultimate goal in dance.
19. The beginning and the ending of a movement phrase are less important than what takes place along the way.
20. Being centered does not mean being located in the middle of a space.
21. Art is, or should be, the province of every human being.
22. An original work of art can never be duplicated with exactness.

23. Technique is the means, not the end.
24. Space is real; it also can be imaginary.
25. Dance coexists with time.
26. Filming is only one way of recording dance; notation is more accurate.
27. Movement varies according to the application of force.
28. Mary Wigman is the originator of modern dance.
29. Dance movement is restricted in accordance with the structure and function of the body instrument.
30. The modern dancer seldom follows the melodic line of the accompaniment; the pulse is more important.

Index

Accompaniment, 24, 29
African dance, 9
Alignment, 13
Asymmetry, 56

Ballet
   classical, 5, 20
   modern, 8, 9
Body instrument
   body type, 13
   efficiency of movement, 11, 12, 13, 25, 33
   fitness, 11, 12, 22
   motor ability, 12
   muscle tone, 12
   structure, 17, 20, 26
   weight control, 12
Breath control, 36

Centered, 35
Class structure
   facilities, 21
   lesson design, 22, 23
   practice costume, 22
   problem solving approach, 24
Communication, 1, 2, 4, 24, 65, 68
Composition, 32, 50-57
Creativity
   contemporary aspect, 4
   image making, 45, 48, 49
   innateness, 43, 44, 46
   observation, 57
   sensory experiencing, 47, 48
Criticism, 17, 24, 35, 50, 67, 68, 69

Dance as art, 3, 4, 5, 8, 9, 19
Dance in education, 9, 10, 18, 19, 20, 75
Delsarte, 31
de Mille, Agnes, 8
Design
   contained design, 53
   definition, 50
   linear design, 51
   simplicity, 55
   structural design, 55
   third dimension, 54
Duncan, Isadora, 5

Energy, 26, 27

Fitness, 22
Floor pattern, 51, 52
Force, 26, 27
Furthering the experience, 10, 75, 76

Graham, Martha, 6, 7, 8, 10
Gravity, 25
Group dance, 23, 45, 46, 57

Holm, Hanya, 7

Improvisation, 39, 49
Individual nature, 24, 31, 43, 44, 46

Jazz dance, 9

Lesson planning, 22, 23
Line, 32, 35, 51

Modern dance
  a temporal expression, 4
  historical development, 6-10
Movement
  combinations, 23, 33
  qualities, 23, 24, 26, 27
Multimedia, 66

Negativism, 17, 18, 21
Notation, 6, 33

Originality, 47, 48

Performing, 61, 62, 63, 64, 76
Placement, 35
Practice, 32, 33, 36
Problem solving, 24, 33, 44, 45

Rhythm, 29, 30, 33, 34
Rites and rituals, 1, 2

Space
  contained space, 53
  imagined space, 28
  neutral space, 27
  real space, 28
  space shaping, 28, 51, 52, 53
Speed, 26, 28
Symmetry, 56

Techniques, 22, 32, 33, 36
Time
  accent, 29
  duration, 28
  emotional or psychological time, 54
  meter, 29
  pedestrian rhythm, 29
  rhythm and counterrhythm, 29

Variety, 55, 57
Volume, 53, 54

Warmups, 22, 23, 33, 34
Wigman, Mary, 6, 7